The Illustrated Olive Farm

CAROL DRINKWATER

photography by

MICHEL NOLL & CAROL DRINKWATER

WEIDENFELD & NICOLSON

Contents

My Adopted Land

When I am not in residence at our olive farm in my adopted land in southern France, husbanding the trees or ensconced in my den, I travel and, from time to time, I give readings or talk at professional events. I relish these outings because they are the occasions that keep me in touch with the impulses of the actress, that creature who comes to life before an audience, who entertains for her bread and butter, or rather the 'Carol' I was before I semi-inadvertently threw it all in to sit here, staring out at the tideless sea, attempting to describe what is around me. Some of the questions most regularly asked of me at these gatherings are: 'What made you do it?' 'Do you regret it?' 'Could you ever picture yourself returning to live in England?' And, without a second's hesitation, I bat back with: 'Love.' 'No, no regrets,' and 'I cannot envisage that day.' It is a fact that I harbour no regrets. *Au contraire*. Still, it has not always been a smooth ride. But even in my darkest hours I have drawn inspiration from the natural beauty surrounding me and I have remained fascinated by Provençal history as well as its language and traditions, many of which reach back into antiquity and one or two of which I am attempting to master, and I have taken heart from the miracle of nature's remarkably regenerative powers.

I share this magical yet shabby home with my French husband, Michel, who I met in Sydney more than a decade and a half ago. I had been selected by one of the British networks to play the leading role in a children's mini-series shooting on location in the Victorian countryside, in and around the old gold-mining towns of Ballarat and Bendigo, two hours' drive north of Melbourne. Michel, who was the executive producer, had never heard of me. Our careers had never crossed. He was operating within the Latin culture and I, in the Anglo-Saxon world. Still, he accepted the choice and a few weeks before I was due to set off he telephoned from Paris to say that he would be on business in London and might he invite me for dinner. At that time, I was performing in the theatre. My dinners were post-show suppers, so we settled on lunch. Unfortunately, two hours before our appointed rendezvous, Michel returned to Paris; a production crisis had called him back. Several weeks later, I flew down under without having made my employer's acquaintance.

Alone in Melbourne, 12,000 miles from home – I was the only cast member who had been shipped in from overseas – working in muddy, uncomfortable conditions, I was delighted

Taken a few months after we met, during a business dinner held on a hired yacht in Cannes.

when Michel's production assistant hauled me off for an elegant dinner at one of the city's many fine restaurants. She spoke of Michel frequently during that evening and I, I can admit it now, was more than a little intrigued by the sound of him, but it seemed that we were destined never to meet. He was due in from Paris to view rushes two weeks after my role was in the can, at which point I flew to Lizard Island off the northern coast of Queensland to dive a strip of the Great Barrier Reef and experience first-hand its fascinating marine life about which I had read so much. Returning south to Sydney, my last port of call before Europe, I checked into The Sebel Town House. This easy-going hostelry no longer exists but in its heydey it played host to the world's entertainment industry – in the suite adjoining mine was Bruce Springsteen! – so it was really no coincidence to discover Michel booked into the same hotel. He rang my room and proposed a drink in the bar. I was finally to make his acquaintance. The magnetism was instantaneous and he invited me to dinner on the following evening. Unfortunately, I was promised at the home of the legendary actress Googie Withers and Michel was leaving for Western Australia the morning after… We bade *au revoir* in the bar, with vague promises of meeting again on an unspecified future occasion in Europe. I was disappointed but I had no intention of bowing out of my soirée with the McCallams. As fate would have it, when I returned to my suite I found a message from Googie cancelling our arrangement. I sped back to reception and scribbled a note for Michel.

Our dinner that following evening proved to be a major turning point in my life. Michel asked me to marry him. *Un coup de foudre.* 'Love at first sight,' he declared shyly. I was speechless. I did not accept but I was deeply attracted to this bearded, blue-eyed stranger. We kissed goodnight in the corridor outside my door and he promised to telephone me from somewhere soon. I remember waking the next morning, wondering if I had dreamed the episode. Until I entered the sun-drenched breakfast room, spied him with three colleagues and he rose at the sight of me.

'I'm flying to Broome in an hour. You haven't responded to my question,' he said, approaching. 'Will you marry me?'

'I don't know,' I grinned.

Cannes TV Festival

Michel was host to television executives visiting the festival. The boat was harboured in Cannes' old port.

'I will call then, if I may?' And with that the handsome if rather unconventional Frenchman had disappeared. It was a heady introduction, a tantalizing opening act, but not one that I allowed myself to take too seriously. My life had been peppered with far-flung encounters. I had acquired a certain professional and, less desired, personal notoriety. I was early-thirties, an independent career woman with not a single tie beyond the next acting contract to fix me and I chose it so. Mine was a carefree and sometimes glamorous existence. It was also solitary but I was not admitting to that. Had I done so I would have been obliged to face the fact that I was wary of inviting any man into my heart, wary of commitment. Make-believe was the stuff of my reality.

For the better part of a decade I had been window-shopping the world for what I described as 'My House by the Sea'. Wherever I worked or journeyed to, I sought opportunities to track down this mythic hideaway. I had no clear concept of my illusory seaside arbour except that it would need to be a far cry from the hustle and bustle of life in my rented flat in north London. An unassuming abode, no doubt, but situated within sight of sea or ocean, bordering a strand where I could stroll, chill out and recharge my batteries after the stresses of urban existence and the actor's perennial struggles for work. I would certainly have required it to be a low-maintenance base with an extremely modest purchase price because I lacked capital. I hadn't saved a penny. All that I had earned I had spent on travels and my actress's peripatetic lifestyle. Over the years I had visited several houses that pleased me, a couple of which were priced within my limited budget, but never one that truly spoke to me. 'My House by the Sea' was, in reality, little more than a chimera, a castle in Spain, an excuse to haunt the world's littorals alone and at my leisure.

Although all talk of marriage between Michel and myself had been gently sidelined, I had met the man I felt I could entrust myself to and our fleeting antipodean encounter had swiftly blossomed into a romance that carried us back and forth on enchanted trips between London and Paris. We had known one another almost six months when he invited me to spend a week with him in the south of France. He was to attend the international television festival held in Cannes in late April. Spring. A perfect season to discover the Côte d'Azur, which I had passed through on several occasions but knew only scantily. I accepted readily.

During those blissfully lighthearted days, while my lover and every other visiting executive cannonaded about the palm-lined Croisette, touching down at meetings, lunches and cocktails, I paddled through the white-sailed hours, swimming, sauntering, daydreaming at the water's edge while bare-footed joggers pounded the spume-darkened sand, observing the corrugated features of locals inert on blue chairs, their copies of the *Nice Matin* sliding from their spreading laps. Or I pressed my face against agency windows conjuring up my elusive waterfront idyll. Without success. Every agent I approached informed me that my paltry budget would buy me less than a postage stamp on the French Riviera. Refusing to be disheartened, I dallied in gothic-dark churches, read about Napoleon's marathon march to Paris embarked upon from here, I shuffled the crowd-pressed alleys of the fruit and veg market, seduced by its multi-coloured hollerings. I remember the aroma of roasting coffee at the portside bars. I remember the streams of dusty water and discarded cigarette stubs running in rivulets along the dawn-scrubbed gutters. I remember the steel of shopfront shutters clunking shut and the street-side bars spilling over with thirsty *commerçants*. Even then I found Cannes meretricious, streetwise. I knew little of its history nor the jewels that lay beyond it. From time to time I would raise my glance, eyes squinting in the sunlight, to gaze at the arena of undulating hills, but I thought not at all about mills or farms or blue damselflies, Bonelli's Eagles, honey bees, hunters, forests of oak, groves of silvery olive trees, and certainly not about pressing drupes into golden oil. All these were to come.

Towards the end of the week an agent telephoned, suggesting that if I set my sights a little further inland he had excellent opportunities on offer. Although Michel and I had not seriously discussed a joint purchase, he entered into the spirit of my quest, and on Saturday morning, his professional commitments completed, we ascended the blossoming hillsides in the company of a slickly attired young snapper, aptly named Mr Charpy, to view his proposed premises, all of which were disappointing. Michel encouraged Charpy to think beyond his own portfolio. 'Surely you know of a forgotten somewhere?' cajoled my new partner. 'An abandoned dwelling nestling in the hinterland.' It did the trick. Charpy recalled two such habitations though he was not representing either. No one was, as far as he knew. The first, broken-brick walls, crumbling behind a fortress-high laurel hedge, was affordable, but lacked a view and did not fire our imaginations. So we hit the road once more, up and down the verdant inclines, in search of the second.

'In times gone by it was a substantial domain producing both olives and vines but most of the land was sold off.' Charpy had not set eyes on the place in an age. 'It has to be four or five years since it was last inhabited.' Our approach was by a serpentine lane at the foot of a pine-clad hill. There were no gates, no fencing, nothing to bar entry or delineate the estate's boundaries. As we began our slow ascent of the tarmacked driveway, an impenetrable jungle flanked us. I can still recall the smell of polished leather from the beige seats in Charpy's Mercedes. The windows were closed – the air-conditioning was on. How I longed to wind down the glass and stick my head out into the wild nature! I can still picture the delicate Wedgewood blue of that spring sky and the dozens of swallows swooping low, as though to warn off the infrequent intruders scaling the gently curving approach. Or possibly they were greeting us.

I will never forget that first sighting of the house: its bold emplacement halfway up the hillside; its fissured, cream façade; its upper-level terrace jagged with broken balustrades that put me in mind of a yawning mouth exposing decayed teeth and, then, one storey beneath, four thorny climbers withering alongside a quartet of pillars. We stepped out of Charpy's sleek saloon into the late morning sun. I took a deep breath. A lifeless almond tree stood sentry by the garage hidden behind a rotting, burgundy-brown rolling door. Soon it would be May. I inhaled myriad softly vernal perfumes rising up from within the undergrowth. There was a deep, deep silence. So silent it resonated. I listened to our footfalls, as we stepped towards the pool. 'There's a swimming pool!' A cracked, bleached-blue oblong crater gaped at us from out of the belly of the earth. It was crawling with straggling strands of ivy and at its deepest recesses brown puddles of rainwater had become clogged with semi-sinking plastic bags. It resembled a rubbish tip more than a pool.

Signs of decay: broken balustraded surround on the upper level and the sorry remains of a swimming pool.

The villa had been constructed by Italians, around the turn of the century, we learned, and christened Appassionata. A musical term meaning 'with passion'.

We free-wheeled around the desiccated climbers obstructing the walkway, which gave off a desultory air. Once upon a time this location must have been so elegant, I was thinking. Once, there would have been life here, vibrancy and laughter. Now the property lay idle. Its doors firmly

*Dead plant-life straddled the long-abandoned villa.
Clearly, though, it had been a handsome house.*

closed on its past, it had been left to the weathers and insects, to galloping nature. Yet, somehow, the house remained lovely and, to my romantic mind, enticing. It faced the distant horizon, proudly, undefeated, full on.

'There will be a view of the Mediterranean from the next level,' whispered Michel, squeezing my hand. Following Charpy, we climbed exterior steps abutting the western wall of the house. A majestic smooth-trunked tree to the left of us as we stepped upwards drew my attention. Its leaves were dark green, large and waxy, with coppery undersides. Aside from 'tree', I had no idea what it might be nor the offerings it had in store for us.

Beyond it lay the fringes of massed plant life, which on that morning appeared as a wall of unidentifiable foliage. Today I know better. The land had been engorged by *garrigue* plants. Sweetly-scented many of them, these indigenous shrubs, including rosemary, rockrose and juniper, thrive on the sunburnt, rocky hillsides rising up behind the Mediterranean shorelines.

I had never heard of cork or holm oaks, nor umbrella pines. I knew nothing of the flora of the maquis. It is a botanist's Elysian field but, to my unknowing eyes, it represented nothing more than a daunting, impenetrable forest of trees, thickets, climbers and thorny green weeds, all of which would take months of hard slog to hack through and clear.

The house itself had been built into the mountainside. Its foundations were embedded in limestone. It had stood on this hillside exposed to the elements for nigh on a century so its structure must surely be sound, I reasoned silently. However, beneath the shallow surface of dry red earth, subterranean rock conduits stored falling rain and channelled it directly to the rear of the house, where it was seeping into the foundations, causing rising damp in every room on the ground floor, but we were not aware of any of this.

'There's a vineyard and the remains of a small cottage over in that direction,' waved Charpy dismissively. 'But, of course, you can't see it. *Beaucoup de travail*,' he muttered disparagingly. How accurate his observation proved to be!

We reached the upper level, a plain cemented deck with its broken balustrades, and turned right in the direction of the balcony, towards a breathtaking view. There, laid out before us, was the tideless tranquillity I had been hungering for. What did I say to myself? That I had come home? That this house in sight of the sea had remained empty, waiting for me? I cannot be sure now.

The asking price was three times higher than my budget. My French was rusty. It had never been fluent. And what on earth was I to do with ten acres of steep, stony jungled land? I was certainly not contemplating olive farming!

I stood gazing out upon the limpid water, towards the two Îsles de Lérins (whose names I did not know then) lying sleepily beyond the bay of Cannes, imbibing the beauty, brushing all considerations aside, assuring myself that this folly of a dream, a decade in the gestating, was plausible. The sun, to the left in the sky above, encouraged my fantasy with its warmth while the man at my side leaned in close, and I smiled, understanding that he was there with me. I think that was the defining moment.

'Why don't we try to find a way in?' Michel set off on a tour of the villa, scrutinizing its rectangular edifice. Charpy hurried after him, arguing that it was impossible for he possessed no keys. But locks had been twisted and forced, rusted membranes of mosquito netting, which protected every aperture, had been ripped from their sockets or cut with knives to facilitate intrusion, while slats from various shutters had been torn away and windows smashed; evidence that the place had been burgled or squatted in the not too distant past.

By comparison, our own breaking and entering was a cinch. Even so, we left the illicit deed to a reluctant Charpy to perform. Charging repeatedly at the solid wood door, heaving his shoulder against it, soiling his pristine navy suit, he eventually released the catch and we made our way into an interior cold, dark and reeking of mildew. The sun had not crept across those walls or *tommette* tiled floors since many a day. Cobwebs swung before us like decomposing stockings on a washing line. Insect husks lay everywhere. We crunched them underfoot. The kitchen at the rear of this upper storey was a disgorged spaghetti of broken machines and perished pipes. There would be no alternative but to rip it all out.

Electricity wires and peeling floral wallpapers drooped everywhere. We flicked at switches, turned taps, nothing operated.

Rewiring. Strip paper. New kitchen, I muttered.

A wide-angle brick fireplace, topped with an extravagantly long pine beam riddled with woodworm, dominated the main living room, *le grand salon*, which was capacious. The remnants of a wood fire as well as a couple of cooking utensils and a bent fork lay in the hearth. In what appeared to be sleeping quarters, the ceilings had been lowered and a curiously narrow plywood corridor with papered shelving had been added. It was out of keeping with the Mediterranean style of the house, created a claustrophic atmosphere and made the walls appear lopsided. It would be painless to remove and, once opened up, the accomodation would have a comfortable, airy feel to it. However, the premises appeared to comprise this one floor containing only two bedrooms. Generous in surface but insufficient for a family home. Were there others? There were, it transpired, but they were one floor below and, bizarrely, there was no interior staircase by which to gain access to them.

We returned to the terrace and descended to the swimming pool level where we noticed another two front doors. Here Mr Charpy, who we had now learned was a qualified notary and was decidedly agitated at the prospect of risking his professional reputation with these unlawful activities, was obliged to repeat his burglar stunt. Once more only, fortunately; both doors opened on to the same three-and-a-half rooms, which we found in a very sorry state of repair. It is difficult to describe the rank stench confined within these long-untrodden corners.

'There is no interior staircase because these rooms would have been intended for beasts,' revealed our agent who then retreated to his Mercedes. I did not know at the time that such a living arrangement is a direct descendant of the ancient Roman style of villa, where the ground floors housed oil mills, wine vats, store rooms and stables. We entered gingerly. The first room was covered, walls to flaking ceiling, with a filthy chocolate-brown carpet that reeked to high heaven. In between this room and the next was a space the size of a large walk-in cupboard housing a loo and extremely basic washing facilities. A runnelled stain, tobacco-coloured, where water had dripped incessantly, streaked the sink's interior. I switched on the tap – there was only the one. It wobbled and squeaked but nothing flowed forth.

Replace all plumbing. New bathrooms and kitchen.

This was not an enterprise for the fainthearted. The villa's entire lower storey would require damp coursing, replastering and… It was hard to know where to begin. I threw a glance in the direction of Charpy's car, knowing that he must be growing impatient. It was gone midday, Saturday, the sacred hour of lunch in France. 'One more quick glance at the view,' I begged of Michel, 'to remind us what is wonderful here.' He and I hared back upstairs, climbing two at a time, passing the monumental tree and hurried to that scene, framed by pine trees, of the sea. 'It's completely insane but I could live here,' I murmured, inhaling the pink blossomed air.

And so it came to be. We scrabbled together the cash, begging and borrowing, to purchase the villa and its acreage in stages and have attacked the renovations over the years. Due to various setbacks, the place remains a long way off completion. As with all such enterprises, there have been many surprises. Aside from a perennial lower ground damp problem and water hassles, most of them have been joyous. Cutting back the land took almost two years, which is to say several attempts. As always with nature, every time we flew off on our busy professional lives the herbage grew up again. Two of the most rewarding revelations for me have been the discovery of the olive trees and learning to farm them, and the Mediterranean itself. What I saw on that Saturday morning of long ago was a sadly forgotten house surrounded by jungled nature overlooking a sea. It might have been any sea. Now I have learnt a little of its personality and its history. The El Dorado I traipsed the world seeking for over a decade has not proved to be the low-maintenance abode where I could chill out and where I would prepare for the next chapter in my actress's urban life. Not at all! Appassionata has become a way of life and a creative act in itself.

Never in my wildest dreams had I entertained maintenance of a farm, particularly with a crop so alien to the world I had grown up in, but once our hillside was cleared and it began to reveal its true personality, what we discovered abiding there on those dry-stone walled terraces were sixty-eight gnarled and weathered, 400-year-old olive trees. It was a magnificent duckling-to-swan revelation. And I was bewitched. Hours, days, months I passed, strolling about the terraces, touching their nobbly trunks, feeling their strength, their longevity, sitting beneath those overgrown ancients at every hour of the day and evening. Each April, I studied and admired their flowers, and throughout the dry, baking summer months of barbecues and guests, I stood amazed as those tiny white-forked flowers shed their minuscule petals and transformed themselves into olive nodes, which

Early autumn in the garden, after the lavender bank (right of arch) has been cut back.

as the year progressed grew fat, oleiferous and a yummy deep purple.

And then as autumn returned, I grew saddened, unable to watch on as the crop dropped to the ground, rotted, and was subsumed into the cracked earth without its offerings tasted. But I did not have an inkling how to harvest these trees or what was to be done with their drupes once they had been gathered. I tried eating one or two but they were bitter, inedible. They needed to be cured, that much I now realized. Or pressed into oil. Yes, olive oil. I bought a manual in French because I could not find one in English, but the language was quite beyond my capabilities at that stage and, in despair, I tossed it aside. As luck would have it, the right man for the job wandered into our lives precisely when we needed him. And from that moment onwards, another journey was underway. One of, oh, so many that this shambling estate has so generously provided me with.

The Olive Farm

The estate comprises ten acres of hillside facing south to the Mediterranean. The lower levels are terraced with drystone walls. Here are the ancient olive groves. Beyond the lane at the foot of the hill lies an olive-groved valley. In olden days, that land was Appassionata's, which is why our caretaker's cottage is across the way and our waterhouse in the valley below.

Water basin

Young olive groves

Second water basin

Ruin in disused vineyard

Magnolia grandiflora tree

One of the drystone walls

Tiled terraces

Ancient olive groves

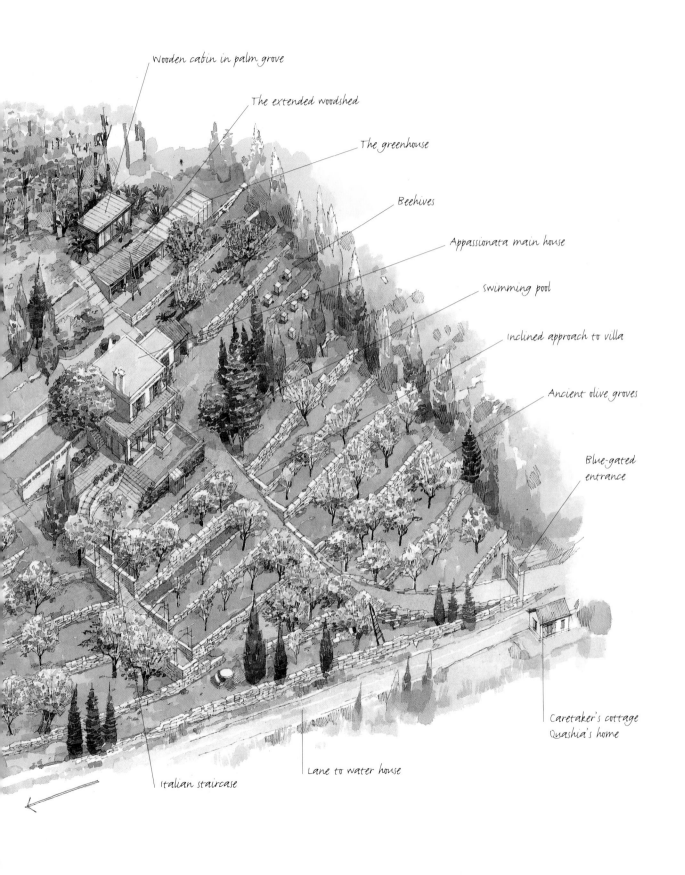

Wooden cabin in palm grove

The extended woodshed

The greenhouse

Beehives

Appassionata main house

swimming pool

Inclined approach to villa

Ancient olive groves

Blue-gated entrance

Caretaker's cottage Quashia's home

Italian staircase

Lane to water house

1 *Creating the Olive Farm*

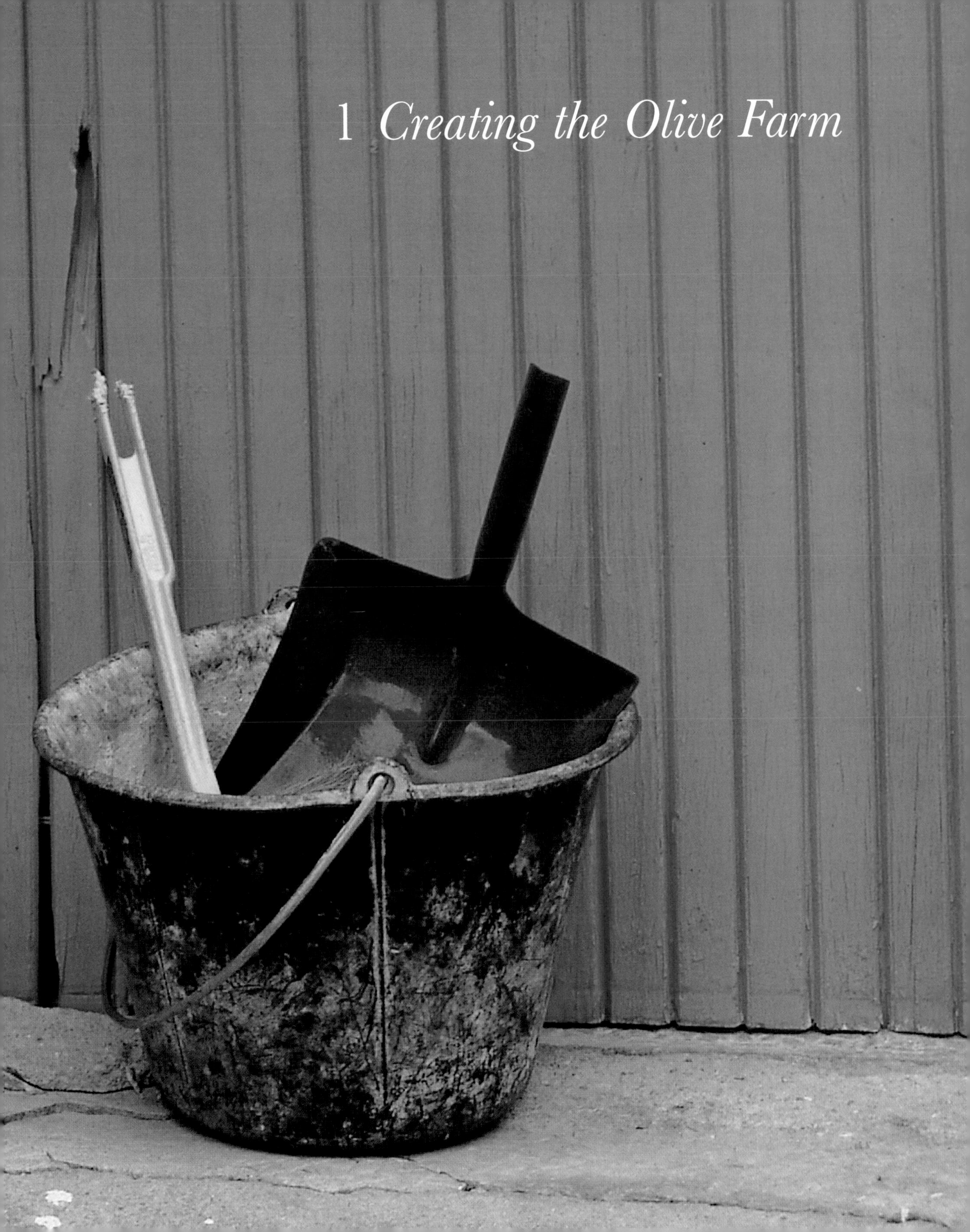

Discoveries and Challenges

We installed ourselves at the property in the baking heat of an early August, accompanied by Michel's twin daughters, Vanessa and Clarisse, along with their rather obese Alsatian, Pamela. Between us we had many dreams and a little over 600 pounds to see us through that first summer of fun and early renovations. Michel had promised the girls, who I barely knew, blissful weeks at our newly acquired villa with swimming pool. They spoke no English – or rather, they kept that skill to themselves – and my inadequate French lacked exercise, but their disappointment upon arrival when they saw the condition of the pool required no translation.

'Don't worry, we'll fill it tomorrow,' Michel reassured them.

Within the hour, we discovered that water and electricity were not available at the flick of a mains switch. The electricity had been cut off. As to the water source, we could not fathom from where it flowed. The temperature was soaring at over 30°C and we were without all basic facilities. A heartening discovery was to learn that every town or village in France, no matter how

Aspects of the house during that first summer. Overgrown, desolate and lacking the basic facilities to begin repairs. I began to wonder if this challenge was beyond us. But the sun shone constantly and Michel's daughters were a delight to discover.

modest, is obliged to supply drinking water, *eau potable*, free of charge. Our first investment was two, twenty-litre canisters, which we filled morning and evening from the fountain in the village. With this we could wash, scrub floors and slake our boundless thirsts.

Meanwhile, Michel battled his way through the dense foliage, up and down the hillside, in search of an elusive well which would provide us with running water. Finally we discovered our source: a distant pumphouse set within an olive grove in a neighbouring valley to which we had right of access. The transportation of water to the brow of our hill remains a very convoluted system but it works – well, most of the time.

Clearing and Planting

High on an endless list of priorities was to dock a patch of land where we could set up a barbecue and read and snooze in the shade. That was the grand plan, but we managed very little relaxing. Clearing around the house proved exhausting. Since our first visit to Appassionata in April, the jungled vegetation had dried in the heat to brittle stalks that clung to our clothes, scratched our bare limbs and was home to clouds of beasties who fed off our sunburned flesh and tormented poor Pamela who sulked in the shade of the cypresses. We were sadly ill equipped but the purchase of more sophisticated tools was beyond our means. So, the girls and I took it in turns to clip with the shears.

To celebrate the arrival of water, I splashed out, not on tools, but on terracotta pots, which I packed with ringlet-headed geraniums, daubing the garden with colour and distracting from the villa's deteriorating edifice.

Far left *The covered walkway alongside the pool in early days – note its crumbling ceiling. That same aspect as it is today. Wistaria in flower surrounds its entrance.* This page *My mother and Michel's parents discovering the cleared land with us and helping me to plant up flower gardens. Michel's father, Robert, was a gifted gardener.* Following pages *The view from a terrace.*

Photos taken over several summers. Left *Michel, me and Henri.* Opposite top and clockwise *Our first summer.* Bottom *Clarisse repainting the shutters.* Bottom right *Michel's father.* Centre left *Michel contemplating the view.*

Novices at Work and Relaxing

Clearing the estate's entire landmass took us more than two years, but during that first summer we eventually managed a strip where we installed table, chairs and parasol – which became too small to shade everyone as the guest count grew! Here we enjoyed market-produce salads and cheeses, local rosé wine and entertaining al fresco.

Friends arrived from London with yet more terracotta pots, which we ceremoniously placed around the empty pool. In fact, once the news was out that we had a 'villa in the south of France', pals descended from various directions. During the first few weeks of occupancy only Michel and I braved the spartan conditions. Without electricity, we had no means of heating water so we showered at the hotel where the we had put Michel's daughters and we brewed coffee on the barbecue out of doors.

Somehow, though, because the sun shone continuously and we were so in love, our world felt luxurious. Indeed, my memories of that first summer are entirely blissful.

Early Days, the Pool

Once we had cleared the pool's basin of ivy skeins and muddied rainwater, we
discovered several cracks. They did not look too sinister, but to be sure I made an
appointment with an expert to inspect the interior and confirm that the cistern
was waterproof. His assessment was fascinating but ultimately disappointing.
In his opinion, our swimming pool had been built before the war, possibly at the
beginning of the 1920s, which would have made Appassionata one of the earliest
of a train of privately owned estates on the Côte d'Azur to boast an outdoor
pool. It was during the twenties, with the arrival of such trendsetters as the
French clothes designer Coco Chanel, that summer holidaying and sunbathing
on the French Riviera became fashionable.

   We need have no concerns about leaks. Our *piscine* was solid but it lacked
any form of filtering system, which in these escalating temperatures meant its
contents would stagnate and turn green from algae within days. 'And the cost of
installing the system?' I enquired. His estimation was more money than we had
provisioned for the entire summer. I think I was more crestfallen than the girls.

From left to right
*Various stages of the pool's
development, shown with
family and Australian friends.
Photo 2 shows Vanessa
walking with Pamela in the
empty basin. Before the basin
was filled Michel ingeniously
used it as an amplifying
system. He placed our little
radio cassette player at its
centre and the music blasted
forth across our hillside.*

We momentarily gave up on the pool dream until a letter reached me informing me that unexpected royalty fees had been paid into my bank. It was such a gift! Works began immediately on the construction of the requisite pumphouse and filter. The pool, with a string of hospepipes, took a fortnight to fill but we paddled and splashed in it anyway, endlessly celebrating its renaissance.

Happiness!
One of my collage spreads of photos from our personal collection taken over several years. This one includes a tiny snap of our wedding in the South Pacific with the Maori chief who performed the service. Alongside it is a rather creased photo taken by Australian Vogue just before we flew off to get married.

Arrival of the Olive Guru

I met René by accident outside the locked gates of a woodmerchant. After such rigorous land clearance we had logs to sell aplenty. He offered me a handsome sum in cash for our chopped stock and then, over a glass of wine in the shade, which has become a ritual of ours, he complimented our olive trees, remarked that they were in need of pruning and asked who looked after them. Nobody, I told him. He proposed himself for the task, at a price. Two-thirds of the rewards were his and one third for us. I argued for a fifty-fifty deal, but he was adamant. René is a wily Provençal. Over the ensuing years he has taught us a great deal about the rudiments of olive farming as well as about the Provençal ways of life.

Right *René with Lucky and Quashia.* Left *Loading his spraying machine with insecticide to spray our trees.* Below *Demonstrating the workings of a new machine that automatically removes leaves from harvested olives.*

Left *René proudly displays his broccoli plants, fed with water flowing freely from the mountains and sourced on the water diviner's land. He comes to visit us laden with gifts of fruit and vegetables.*

Until his retirement, he was a lorry driver, proprietor of his own vehicle. During the Second World War, he used to transport black-market comestibles the length of the coast, and from Monaco 'where they paid handsomely' inland to Lyon, where he had a nightclub chanteuse as mistress.

René always falls on his feet and his tales of triumph are delightful. These days he works on an estate owned by a water diviner who boasts impressive olive groves. There, where the water flows in abundance and free of charge, René grows his fruit and vegetables. The produce is of award-winning proportions. He brings us basketloads as gifts and then in the next breath charges me for a product he has taken from our garage!

Our one real point of disagreement is whether or not to spray the olive trees. I am against it whereas he would rain down any poison on the land if he thought there was profit to be made.

Left *Quashia, our very loyal gardener. Rabah, his sheep dog. Rabah was Quashia's herder when he was an adolescent shepherd. He told me how he frequently left the dog alone with the sheep overnight in the mountain pastures because the animal was such a trustworthy guard. And then one morning Quashia found his beloved companion dead. He says he cried for weeks. Our loyal friend has carried this photo of Rabah with him ever since, for more than fifty years.* Right *Quashia prefers to stand to attention, like a soldier, when his photo is being taken.*

Quashia, Our Loyal Gardener

Our professional commitments require Michel and me to travel frequently. These absences mean we must rely on someone else to take responsibility for the estate. Quashia is our man. He used to work pruning the orange groves and cutting the grass on a neighbour's holding and I frequently remarked how handsome that land looked. By trade he was a mason and helped us out once when we needed a fence built in a hurry. Before retirement he turned his skilled hands to gardening. Fortunately, when the neighbour moved away, we were able to offer Quashia a home with us.

He mends the tumbling drystone walls and tends the animals and olive groves with a passion equal to our own. Quashia is the soul of our olive farm. Although he has lived in France since he was fifteen he is originally from the Constantine

countryside of Algeria. His second wife and family remain there. He boasts four sons, two daughters and, to date, thirty-one grandchildren to whom he returns, laden with presents, twice a year.

When we are hard at work gathering the olives from the nets, in preparation for the pressing at the mill, he recounts stories of his childhood in war-torn Algeria. He lost his father when he was twelve. His older brother was in France, earning

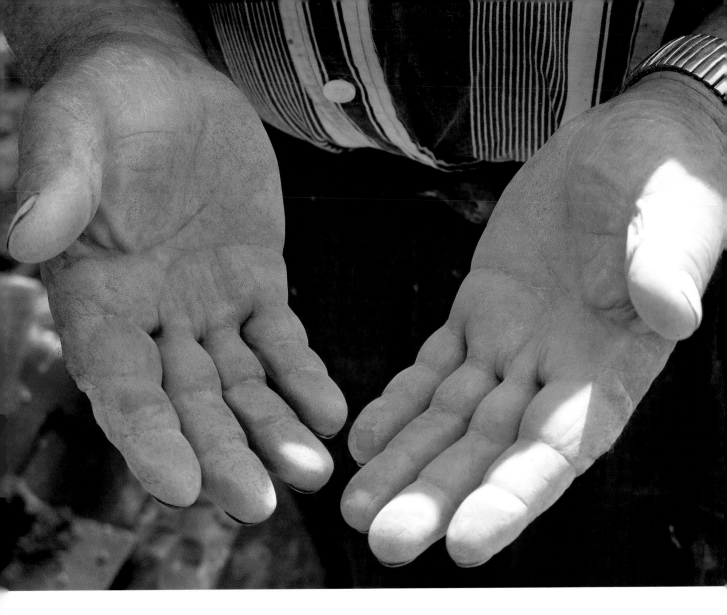

money to send back home so Quashia became the head of the family. It was during the Algerian war with France. One day French soldiers came and burned all they possessed: two barns. Quashia took off for the mountains to collect and cut wood. This he carried on his back, like a donkey, all the way to the city to sell at the market in order that he could buy food for his bereaved mother and his younger siblings. He made those mountain excursions regularly and with this modest income he constructed his family a new home, which, he boasts, is still standing today. He and his wife inhabit yet another house he built.

Our gate and hand-built stone pillar entwined with oleander and plumbago blossoms.

Walls, Terraces, Tiles and Pots

Michel has an exceptional eye for structure and colour. He also possesses a boy scout's instinct for where to find what is required. I would have shopped for what was needed at local stores. Not Michel. He took us hunting along the coast and hinterland, scouring forgotten antique yards and cobbled courtyards piled high with bric-à-brac.

The terracotta tiles that pave our terraces and steps are reclaimed. They are almost impossible to find nowadays but we were fortunate. We chanced upon crates of them in yet another bric-à-brac yard, whereupon Michel instantly reserved the entire consignment.

'We'll never use all these,' I moaned. But we did, and I only wish we could find more.

This page *Drystone walls, known locally as* en restanque. Above *Quashia repairing a wall.* Right *Pots from Crete, Africa and* (upper left) *locally fired, roof tiles we have used for restorations and tiled floors we discovered buried beneath cement in the guestrooms.*

Practically all the balustrades surrounding the house were damaged. Their shape is dissimilar to others used hereabouts, so finding a mason to replace them proved nigh on impossible. Michel grew obstinate in his determination to remain faithful to the original design and not exchange them for others, more readily available. Eventually, he found a mason who knew where a mould might be created. Each balustrade requires twenty-four hours to set. Our order, for over 200, meant that one mould would take six months and more to deliver the required number. Finally, after extended negotiations with the canny mason, Michel agreed to purchase six moulds. Expensively. With that, our terrace restoration was achieved in a single summer.

In later years, when we needed further balustrades for a new wall, I called the man to retrieve our moulds. (At the time, he had insisted on storing them himself.)

We travelled three hours in scorching midsummer to visit this collection of chateau artifacts and ironwares (above left), *searching for a gate. Ours* (right) *was a rusty old thing. I dismissed it, but Michel assured me it was just what we needed. 'Wait till it is painted the blue of the shutters.'* Following pages *Our balustrades.*

They have been destroyed, he announced, refusing to pass on to me the specialist who had created them. After many harassed weeks of searching, I finally found a merchant who agreed to make a new mould if I brought along an example for the work required. It took two days for a workman to dig one of the balustrades out of our original wall. When I arrived at the stone merchants the surprised proprietor said: 'These are rare but, fortunately, I have six moulds of this very design.' I stared at him in amazement and gave him our name. He laughed loudly. Needless to say we never worked with the mason again.

Turquoise on Blues

Coastal Provence is renowned for the painters who have sojourned here, captivated by the light's changing hues at every moment of the day. The predominant colours of the landscape are the sky's cobalt blue, the sea's fluid jades, the vegetation's viridescent and silvery greens and the rich burned red of the earth: colours as old as time. When we bought here, I was oblivious to these palettes as well as to the textures that give this or, indeed, any region its personality. Michel opened my eyes to 'seeing' in this way. The blue tiled roof of Henri Matisse's chapel at Vence was his inspiration for the vibrant blue of our woodwork.

Michel felt that it would be more interesting to paint the insets of the shutters and doors turquoise. The colour marries well with the Matisse blue we had chosen: it lifts the woodwork so that it does not appear as a block of blue and it gently reflects our land and seascapes.

Fascinated by Olive Trees

The olive tree embodies the history of a civilization, that of the Mediterranean and its diverse peoples. From the eastern coast of our ancient sea to its western shores, the olive tree is farmed: 800 million of the 900 million olive trees cultivated in the world today are growing around the perimeter of the Mediterranean. The farming of the tree, harvesting, pressing the olives to oil, its uses in the kitchen and as medicine, olive festivals, even the commerce linked to it, are intrisically threaded into the web of Mediterranean cultures. Each of the three major monotheistic religions of the Mediterranean basin – Christianity, Judaism and Islam – revere it as a sacred tree and cite it in their scriptures.

As a rule, these gnarled old survivors live for centuries, but there are examples throughout the Mediterranean basin of trees that have already celebrated their first millennium. Even more astounding, there are trees in Lebanon that have been carbon dated to several thousand years old. The olive tree can withstand searing heat and frosts as low as –7°C. It can be burnt down, chopped to its base, suffer its

Previous pages *Path through an olive grove on St Honorat, off the coast of Cannes.*
Left *Ripening fruits on one of our* cailletier *trees. The olive branch is an international symbol of peace.* Following pages *Ancient trees on our land. Every one is different, each gnarled and twisted in its own way. When our land was cleared for the first time, we discovered sixty-eight of these ancient trees, all in urgent need of pruning. Today, these dappled groves shade us from the heat as well as feeding us.*

trunks to explode due to extreme cold and it will still regenerate, which is why it is called the tree of eternity.

Its life-giving properties are world-renowned. From a bitter, inedible fruit comes a smooth golden oil which is exquisite to taste. The food it gives us in the form of marinated fruits or oil for cooking and salads have more health-giving properties than almost any other single food product. It is believed to protect against several cancers. In ancient times its leaves were steeped and the liquid drunk to lower high blood pressure and control blood sugar levels.

It is the tree of life and the staff of life. It is a corner-stone of ancient Western nutrition, a jewel at the centre of the Mediterranean heritage. Few doubt the claim that the olive was the first tree to be cultivated, but where precisely that discovery took place and how it came about remains a tantalizing mystery.

In antiquity, the wood of the olive was much sought after but it was difficult to come by because certain ancient cultures forbade the chopping down of an olive tree – a capital crime. It makes exquisite furniture and burns slowly to keep us warm. Here, in southern France, it is illegal to destroy an olive tree.

A well-pruned olive tree, so the Provençal saying goes, is one a swallow can fly through without brushing the tips of its wings against the branches. The trees need plenty of air and light to avoid fungal infections and to lessen the risk of incubating insects in the heat. Above *Quashia attacks a tree, clearing out the dead wood first.* Right *Jacques, our swimming pool expert, our beekeeper and Quashia debate pruning methods.*

Pruning

Once our land had been cleared, we discovered, planted in rows along
the drystone terraces, sixty-eight twisted olive trees. René told me that these
ancients are over four hundred years old. He also warned us that they were
in urgent need of pruning. They were not in danger of dying, but they were
wild and unhealthy and pruning them would regulate the trees' production.

There are two methods of pruning olive trees. The first is to cut the
branches evenly, creating a round head. This delivers a neat, pretty tree,
ornamental, but it does not yield a significant crop. The second is to cut the
crown low by lopping the shoots growing heavenwards. This gives the tree a
flattish top and takes away height. An olive never bears its fruit in the same
place – usually its yield appears on the previous year's branch growth so the
lower branches are left long, allowing them to fall earthwards, loose, floating
like swirling silver skirts. This method returns quality and quantity of fruit
and it is a magnificent sight to see, particularly at sunset when the golden
rods of light stream through the pendulous argentine limbs.

Spraying, to ward off pests. I am against it but some years it is unavoidable. The notion of organic farming is relatively new to the olive-farming community here in France. Thankfully, there is a growing awareness of the dangers of excessive use of insecticides.

Spraying

Several insects attack olives, but our greatest enemy in this part of the world is the *mouche d'olive*, the olive fly. It burrows its way into the base of the developing fruit until it eventually destroys the crop. As yet, no reliable organic deterrent has been discovered to combat it, so we are occasionally obliged to spray the trees with a chemical insecticide. Each year, the Chambre d'Agriculture informs us of the current level of olive-fly risk and suggests which sprays to use. The general practice here usually involves inundating the crops with insecticide four times a year during the summer months. I tend to choose to spray only when the telltale sign – a black bruise on the base of the drupe – warns me that the fly has infiltrated the groves. Some years, we don't spray at all. These are the years when our olive oil is organic.

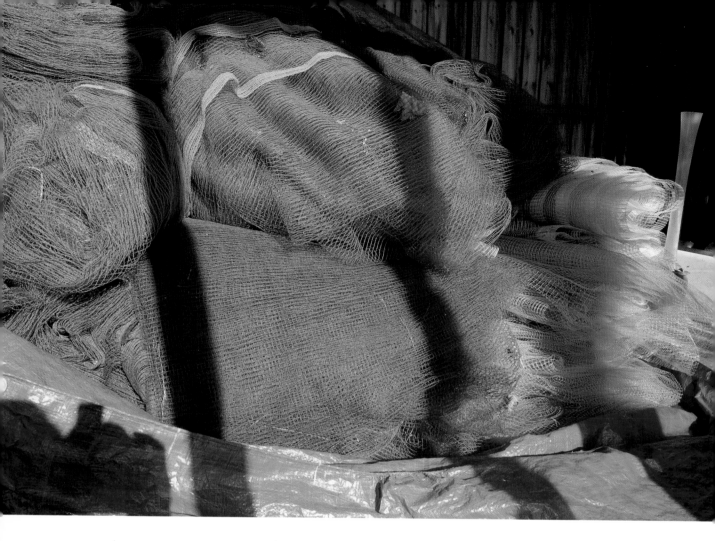

If the weather is warm, I leave the washed crates to dry in the sun. As our yield from the groves expands, I am forever buying more crates. They are usually made in Italy, of a solid plastic, and hold around twenty to twenty-five kilos of fruit. Counting the filled crates is an efficient way of knowing approximately how many kilos of olives have been gathered.

Preparations for Harvest

As autumn begins to fold into winter and the drupes on the trees have grown
fat and purply, we begin our preparations for the olive harvest, *la cueillette*.
In the Provençal diary, gathering commences on 25 November, the feast of Ste
Catherine Labouré, but, of course, this is flexible. It depends on the readiness
of the fruit and the farmer's preference for the taste of his oil. Olives can be
harvested green, piebald or black. Each produces a distinct flavour. We tend to
pick ours when they are turning from green to piebald. There is marginally less
oil in these early-season fruits, but the flavour and quality is first-class delivering
a creamy, yet sharpish, peppery-tasting oil. Ours has been described by the AOC
experts as 'almond-flavoured'! Mauve fruits produce oil that is corn-yellow while
harvesting the drupes much later in the season – black fruits that have ripened on
the trees until late January or February – produces more oil and with a taste that
it is mustier, almost mushroomy.

Ours is a single-variety estate, which means that we grow only one variety of olive
tree on our small farm. It is the *cailletier*, also known as the Olive of Nice. These trees

The weather in this season can be unpredictable. Come rain or shine the nets must be laid. If conditions are stormy, it is all the more urgent to cover the ground. Heavy rain can beat the fattened drupes off the branches, and if the olives are not in the nets, the gathering is more time-consuming because you are obliged to root about amongst grass and earth in search of the buried fruit.

produce smallish fruits but of an exceptional quality both for making oil and for consumption as table olives. Before the harvesting can begin the ground encircling the trees needs to be cut and cleared so that the nets we are about to lay are not cluttered with grass tufts and stones. The nets and the crates have spent the year in storage. While the men roll out the nets and lay them around the feet of the olive trunks – to catch the falling drupes – I wash and air the red crates. They are used for storing the gathered fruit and transporting the kilos to the press, so it is essential that they are spotlessly clean.

Harvesting

Harvest time. *La olivaison*: the olive season. Harvest time is an intense, joyous period and a very social one. Friends and neighbours will drop by to lend a hand with the work. The olives are collected from the nets on hands and knees – it is backbreaking and destroys my nails! Fruits fall naturally or we ascend into the boughs and shake them gently, coaxing the ripe drupes earthwards. We never beat the olives off the trees with sticks because it bruises the fruit. The Italians have invented a machine that rather resembles a fist of vibrating iron fingers on a pole. The pneumatic harvester claws the fruits directly from the branches, clearing a tree that is heavy with approximately 170 kilos of olives within the hour.

The gathering is physically debilitating. It is an excellent time for Quashia and Michel to bond. Occasionally, I leave them to it or friends drop by to lend a hand. Previous pages *This tree is laden with over a thousand kilos of fruit.*

It is true that these machines are extremely time and labour efficient, but they are also rather expensive and, I fear, might damage the fruit, although the claim is that the combing action of the pneumatic fingers causes relatively little bruising to the drupe. Our holding is too modest to justify the expenditure for such a contraption but, in any case, I am old-fashioned in that I relish the traditional methods and the contact with nature. On a good day we can hope to pick clean two trees: 300 kilos of fruit, if we are lucky. The time involved means that we are out of doors for extended hours. We talk only intermittently, concentrating on the work, but I enjoy the birds, listening to their songs. There are usually still plenty

The dogs enjoy the harvesting activities. They frolic on the nets, getting in my way, growing overexcited by the continuous activity. Below Bassett finds himself caught under a net and cannot fathom a way out. Previous pages Hand-picking from the tree.

of butterflies about too. My task, these days, is to collect the fallen puddles of fruit and pack them into the crates. I have given up on climbing the ladders.

Frequently the weather in late November is gloriously sunny, so when friends come to help we will picnic outside in true French rural fashion, with our wooden table laden with bottles of wine and cheeses and torn hunks of fresh bread. That, too, is part of the experience, the camaraderie. Harvesting is a group activity that has been acted out over millennia and it pleases me to participate in it, to keep faith with our Mediterranean past.

Snow is exceptionally rare in our southerly region, but this year it has fallen heavily and has obliged us to postpone the gathering. This will delay our preparations for the mill. Below Lola *experiencing snow for the first time.*

Snow! It is only the second time in almost two decades that snow has fallen this close to the coast. Beautiful as the landscape looks, it will halt our harvest and, perhaps, damage our crop. From the moment the olives have left the trees they begin to oxidize. If they are not pressed without delay, our oil will be acidic and it will have a bitter taste. Our task is to get the fruits from the trees, from the nets into crates, all detritus such as leaves and stones and twigs sorted and thrown out, and drupes delivered to the mill to press within six days of gathering. The heavy snowfalls mean that there are shoals of fruit lying in the nets, wrinkling.

Mill Preparations

The continuing bright sunshine has melted the snow. The earth is damp from such an excess of flowing water but we are able to continue gathering olives. Many have grown as wizened as prunes while others have been gobbled up by hungry birds, leaving just the stones. We rise before dawn and begin our day at 4am. If we are to meet our rendezvous at the mill, we will need to catch up on lost time. Quashia is out on the land where he continues with the picking, while Michel and I are sorting through the crateloads of fruits. It is against the European standards of hygiene to deliver olives that have not been *trié*, selected. The miller will not accept deliveries

Once the snow has melted away and we can begin gathering again, our days commence at 4am. We need to catch up on lost time. Above I am calling from the window: Le café est pret! Coffee's ready. *Right* Michel, *tired, lacking sleep and coffee.*

that are muddled with leaves, twigs and small stones because it damages his machines. Our sifting takes place in the garage and the summer kitchen where the laden crates are stored because these areas are cool and lack humidity. I have the task of turning the olives twice a day to keep them dry. We always keep one crate empty to pour olives into. This way the olives are rolled and moved and aerated. If they remain packed tightly together, humidity sets in which creates mould. I can smell it – a perfume of damp mushrooms – as soon as I walk into the darkened room. At all costs the drupes must be kept dry or the taste of the oil will be altered as well as its acid content. We are working to keep the acid content of our oil below 0.8 per cent. Any higher and we would not be producing oil that is extra virgin.

To the Mill

Usually I drive alone to the mill. I look forward to these visits, watching the day rise across the verdant valleys and the glinting wintery sea. The village where our mill is situated is high up in the hills behind Grasse. I take the curves cautiously because any unexpected swing around the corkscrew bends would send all our laboriously gathered fruit flying. If I am early – the mill opens at 7.30am – I walk up into the silent village to the boulangerie and buy three *pains au chocolat*: one for myself and the other two for the miller and his pretty wife. Our mill is a family-run enterprise. Now that the old miller, Christophe, has retired, Gérard, his son, and Gérard's wife run the business. The season is short – four months at the

Top *Ancient stone pressing wheel.*
Right *Pouring our fruit into the
weighing crate.* Lower left *Typical
French farming vehicles.* Lower right
*After the drupes have been washed.
I am preparing them for their shunt
along the conveyor belt.*

outside – and all the farmers, who descend from miles in every direction to one of
twenty-seven olive mills operating within the Alpes-Maritimes districts, insist upon
their appointments for pressing at more or less the same time, so we must book
well in advance. Unfortunately, the vagaries of weather and harvest difficulties –
this year's snow – can upset any farmer's schedule. What makes our situation all
the more urgent is that oil bearing the coveted AOC label must be pressed within
six days of harvesting or it loses that honoured designation.

Upon arrival I empty our crateloads into even larger crates, which are wheeled
into the chilly subterranean mill area. Here, they are weighed. Then begins the

process of transforming the drupes into satiny golden oil. The drupes are washed and shunted along a conveyor belt into a machine that churns and presses them into a thick dark paste. The water and oil are then separated out and the dried paste is set aside for use as fuel; what remains is pure, cold-pressed olive oil.

Awaiting our new season's produce can be tense. I pass the time studying the farmers' faces and eavesdropping on their conversations. Their earnest discussions are centred around the business of oil farming or the cost of living in modern-day France. I smile, but while we wait we are anxious, wondering whether this year our yield will be top quality. Other farmers arrive. One of the joys of coming here is observing the farmers' arrivals with their mounds of olives. At first glance their fruit might appear robust, healthy and clean but an inch or so beneath the surface can be found an assortment of rubbish, particularly tiny stones which, of course, weigh heavily. If their mounds are, unlike ours, to be added to a cooperative pressing they will recoup a disproportionate amount of oil by weight to the olives they have delivered.

In the early days the farmers regarded me with a suspicious eye, but now that

The long wait. Sad-eyed, worried, intense: I take great delight in observing the farmers and eavesdropping on their conversations. Their faces are so very expressive.

Left *Gérard, the miller, is decanting our oil.* Right *A concerned farmer is checking the quality of his produce.* Bottom *The scales used to weigh each container of oil.* Previous pages *Our newly pressed liquid gold.*

we have gained an AOC, they don't know what to make of me. Our miller presses oil for over a thousand farms. Only four have been awarded an AOC and of those four we are the only non-Provençals.

While I am gazing about or deep in thought, Gérard signals to me. Our oil is almost ready. When that first gush of oil comes spluttering forth from the tap, it is a thrilling and very satisfying moment. Gérard nods his approval. 'First class,' he concludes. I slip my finger under the spray and lift the savoury liquid to my lips. Smooth, crisply golden, like perfect honey. All our labouring has been worthwhile.

Bottling in the Garden

Our harvest is usually completed by Christmas. Bottling in the garden is an annual winter activity. December and January, dark-tunnelled months in so many northern European countries, are habitually warm here. On the wooden table beneath the *Magnolia grandiflora* tree we line up rows of empty, clear-glass bottles. These we have been collecting all year for this purpose. We do not filter our oil, so any tiny particles of olive flesh that remain after the pressing stay floating within the liquid. It is possible to buy filtered or unfiltered olive oil, we prefer it the authentic way. The oil has a thicker, cloudier consistency but it is richer in flavour, and none of the nutrients, the goodness, found in the olive fruit have been removed.

It is oil at its most natural, and finest.

Decanting is a simple process but usually takes two of us as spilling the oil would be a crime. Following pages Our recently pressed oil bottled in the sunlight.

Left *Young trees grown from cuttings.* Top right *Trees used exclusively for propagation.* Lower right *A sign pointing to the alleys of* cailletiers, *which is the variety we farm, otherwise known as the Olive of Nice.*

The Nursery

Several years back, after our very first pressing at the mill, we were advised that the quality of oil produced by our centuries-old trees was exceptionally high and we might want to consider putting our oil forward for an 'AOC'. AOC is an abbreviation of Appellation d'Origine Controllée. It is the highest honour awarded in France to comestible produce, their benchmark of quality. Outside France, it is most regularly seen on their finer quality wines. If a label declares an AOC then you can be reassured that what you are purchasing is a first-class vintage.

We decided to give the suggestion a go, but what we did not know at the time was how rigorously the French protect the labels of prestige they award to their various food products, nor what a journey lay ahead for us if we were to try to gain this recognition. The first hurdle we had to overcome

Top *Trainee gardeners at work.*
Centre *Olives growing on saplings.*
Bottom *A very tiny* cailletier.
Opposite *Propagators, their trunks
have been netted against rabbits.*

was the addition to our estate of
young trees. The French Chambre
d'Agriculture states that a holding needs
to husband a minimum of 250 trees
before it can be classed as an *oliveraie* –
olive farm. Even with the sixty-four
goliaths we were alreading farming plus
a few other fellows way up the top of the
hill that we had not even attempted to
prune for fruit, we were well below the
requisite figure. I set off to enquire after
prices at our local garden centre but soon
learned that AOC-quality trees cannot
be purchased from any local nursery.
There are *pépinières* in every olive-growing
region in southern France which have
been controlled and approved by
agricultural representatives of the state.
These nurseries are classified as
propagators of top-quality olive trees.

The word *pépinière* is derived from *pépin*
which translates as fruit pip. A *pépinière* is
a seed bed or a nursery. Perhaps it was,
once upon a time, used to describe a seed
merchant? Today, of course, such

merchants are the nurseries, the garden centres themselves.

I had never asked myself how an olive tree is propagated. I know that it can live forever and is relatively slow to reach maturity but, with patience and many years to hand, might we succeed in growing trees from the stones of our olive fruits? The answer is no. Fascinatingly, if an olive tree is propagated from a stone it reverts back to its original small, inedible fruited, wild variety; its primeval state.

No cultivated variety can be propagated from a stone. Aside from buying

trees I was interested to learn how we might reproduce them ourselves. It is possible to transplant a sucker, one of the many that shoot up from the base, the exterior root, of a mature tree. We have successfully experimented with this method and now have several thriving junior trees on our grounds, rooted from cuttings. They appear to be prospering, but whether they will ever produce fruit of any quality remains to be seen. Indeed, we cannot be sure that they will produce any fruit at all. I am keen to find out!

ONIOL, the organization that oversees the planting of virgin *oliveraie* or the

Opposite *Olive trees do not require endless amounts of water. They are irrigated once every three weeks.* This page *Michel is examining the quality of the youngsters before placing an order. A tractor is used to transport the wooden crates packed with young trees.*

extension of existing groves, sent us a list of nurseries from which we were obliged to purchase our trees. The nearest was in the hinterland behind Hyères, deep in the heart of the Var, AOC wine country, a drive of approximately two hours. This particular garden centre produces one hundred and eighty *thousand* olive trees a year, of thirty-six different varieties. Strolling through their olive fields, on a baking hot summer's day, with the mountains of Maures as a backdrop was a spectacular sensation for me. As far as the eye could see in any direction was a silver sea of tender young olive trees, varying in size from tiny twiglets to others ready for purchase as three-, six- or nine-year-olds. Michel placed an extremely modest order on our behalf for 200 six-year olds.

Planting

Olive groves thrive best on hillsides with shallow and low fertility soils. Our land is the ideal terrain for the olive tree and I gratefully thank those who worked so hard in years gone by to create our drystone walls. However, planting saplings into a hill that is basically solid limestone rock proved backbreaking work. Witnessing this tremendous effort, I suggested that this act of planting should be celebrated. So I sent out invitations, welcoming friends and family to plant a tree, drink a glass of champagne with us and ceremoniously christen each tree. The trees are shooting vigorously though they will not yield fully until they are fifteen to twenty years old. Still, it gives me enormous satisfaction to gaze up the hill and know that long after Michel and I have passed on and our love story on this farm has been forgotten, generations beyond us will reap the fruits of our labour of love.

In Provence, it is said that a 100-year-old olive tree is still a baby. Therefore, the planting of olive trees is a gift to the future, to the patrimony of Provence and the Mediterranean. *Opposite* Our 200 trees before planting. *Opposite right* Hans from East Berlin plants a tree with me. *This page* Michel and Quashia dig every hole themselves. *Previous pages* For those who can afford it, the nursery sells mature trees. These could be anywhere between 80 and 150 years old.

2 Living on the Olive Farm

Living on the Olive Farm

My original search had been for a House by the Sea. Once Michel and I had finally purchased this old farm, Appassionata, and set to work on the structural necessities, we then became side-tracked by the olives and the natural gifts we discovered here. During all those years of backbreaking work and serious financial adversity, it was all too easy to forget that what I had set my heart on was a coastal idyll, a hideaway where I could write as well as, quite simply, build a home to chill out in. I had always dreamed of an environment which could be perceived as a corner of paradise, where dogs ran about freely, music played continuously, where friends and families were always welcome and could gather together to relax, swim, eat fresh fruits picked directly from the orchards and lend a helping hand to create with us plates of fresh or, even better, organic foods, consumed around our long wooden table.

Left *Old chairs that I bought from bric-à-brac markets and Michel has painted bright colours.* Right *Walkway to the pool and guest bedrooms, with Bassett, our hunting dog, sleeping in the shade.*

Fruits of the Land

When we arrived here, although we could not see them beneath the jungle of overgrowth, there existed a range of fruit trees. Once revealed, we found that most were surviving but were in bedraggled condition, strangled by a might of creepers, struggling with little light and no irrigation aside from occasional rain. Several, though, appeared long dead, which was certainly the case with the tiny orange grove situated alongside the swimming pool. The six trees looked like nothing more than perished logs standing upright. The estate agent told us they had been killed off the preceding winter by harsh frosts. At the end of our first summer we cut them back, sheer to the ground, intending to plant new stock at some later stage. Extraordinarily, they began to sprout tender lime-green shoots

Opposite *The orange grove alongside the pool. Defunct when we bought the farm, today it flourishes.* This page *We harvest the oranges in February. Michel picks the fruit from the trees while I sort out those that are worth preserving.* Previous pages *Washed figs from the garden drying in the sunshine.*

alongside their deadwood bases. I think this was one of the earliest examples I encountered here of the force of nature, its dogged determination to fight back. We left the suckers and, lo and behold, within a year they had sprung up into small trees. Slender and delicate as they appeared, they were being nourished by well-established root systems. Still, Michel doubted they would ever bear fruit. Today, they are as robust as they must once have been, perhaps more so because they are regularly pruned and cared for. Their oranges are bitter fruits, not intended for eating. We use them for marmalade or sliced into drinks as a refreshing alternative to lemon. René carts away boxes of them,

Opposite *Apple orchard planted in memory of my father.* This page *From one lemon tree we could fill the pool with lemonade. We use these citruses in salad dressings, with all fish dishes and stuffed inside roast chickens.*

returning with flagons of sweet wine. And in spring, when the buds unfold into white blossom, their scent like a song drifts across the garden. I marvel that all this has been given to us from a few lifeless timbers.

Apples are not indigenous to this seaside neighbourhood. I planted our small mixed-variety orchard in memory of my father. I cherish a childhood souvenir of a house we never actually moved into but where my parents toiled enthusiastically in the garden at weekends. It was a modest patch of land but on it grew forty apple trees. My father always seemed content there. It was one of the few places I experienced him at peace as a family man, and, because he loved the grounds of Appassionata, sitting, strolling, reddened by the sun, I resolved to plant an apple tree as shade for him. But I became so consumed with work that I never got around to buying the sapling. When he died I planted two young trees: the first t o honour my undelivered promise and the second in celebration of him. I have

planted another every year since. He died in a June but I hold back until November, 'when all wood takes root', our planting season. His favourites were the crisp Granny Smiths and, curiously, that is the tree that dominates his tiny orchard. It shoots up with the zest of youth. When I trim it back – I have become quite adept at apple pruning – I recall those childhood weekends in Kent.

Our sole lemon tree is a *Citronnier des Quatre Saisons*, which means that it fruits all year round. I bought it to to cheer up a rather unattractive area around the garage and stables, but it very quickly outgrew its pot and so I transferred it into the ground on one of the spacious south-facing terraces. I was ignorant of the fact that a mature, healthy lemon tree can produce anywhere between one to two thousand lemons a year. We are inundated! 'Organic lemons, anyone?' One day soon, I will begin to serve homemade lemonade and meringue tarts.

We have fig trees everywhere, many self-seeded. The master of them all overhangs the swimming pool. A twisted, grey-trunked rhinoceros of a beast, it might have grown up in the Garden of Eden. In late summer, a glut of its sticky, bleeding offerings spatter the driveway and leave greedy guests locked in the bathroom.

René and the secrets of Vin d'Orange

René no longer manages our olive groves. He has found another more lucrative arrangement than ours. In any case, I felt that it was time for us to take over the reins of our own smallholding. We could never agree about the efficiency and principle of spraying the crops, and I always seemed to owe him money! This amicable, professional separation has not dented our friendship, which remains firm and convivial. He still holds keys to the gate and it tickles him pink to 'have access to an actress's door'. René is a ladies' man and a frightful flirt. I came home once to find him splashing about in the pool with a lady friend. He was not in the least fazed. 'You don't mind, do you? We were hot,' was his explanation before requesting that I uncork a chilled bottle of his *vin d'orange*.

One of René's greatest pleasures is to drop by for 'un petit verre', a glass of something cool, preferably in the shade. He always has a tale to tell and he usually comes bearing gifts from the land.

The production of alcohol is as carefully controlled in France as every other agricutural by-product. The law states that only one manufacturer in each village has the right to distil spirits. René takes great pride in flaunting this regulation and quite openly boasts about it. Orange wine does not qualify as alcohol. As far as I am aware anyone can produce it as long as it is for personal consumption. All that is required is the recipe, which is not that easy to come by I have discovered. After René began husbanding our olives, he suggested that he also harvest the oranges. In return for the entire crop he would supply us with marmalade and orange wine. Having no other plans for these bitter citruses, I agreed. He returned with two jars of marmalade, which I have to admit is the best I have ever tasted, and a couple of bottles of sweet orange wine. I asked him for the recipes. He shook his head and declared them a family heirloom.

Almond Growing

Acquaintanceship with our almond tree came a little after the olives and oranges. A twisted veteran, it clings for dear life, at a most precarious angle, to a drystone wall. Certain that it was going to plunge forward, taking with it the walled terrace beneath, I said we should fell it, that it was a hazard, but Michel refused. I am happy that we left it because no such disaster occurred and it continues to grow happily and produce its fruit, which it never crossed my mind to do anything with, city girl that I am.

It blossoms before any other tree, an exquisite powder pink. It is the delicate messenger of spring. I think that was really the only recognition I gave it, until summer. Early one morning – when we were sitting on the upper terrace enjoying our breakfast coffee – we noticed the branches of the Italian cypresses flexing. The spectacle of a hunting party of red squirrels springing as though on trampolines across the tall pointed trees, intent upon the almond, was quite a sight. Lined up, waiting their turn, bouncing gently, they looked like athletes at the starting gate. They took it in turns – a pair at a time – to leap to the almond (no mean distance) where they gathered its green, fur-skinned nuts and then departed, leaving place for their companions. I was astounded at how well mannered they were with one another. Why aren't we collecting the nuts? I found myself asking.

Below right *The almond tree growing at right angles out of a drystone wall.* Above from left to right *The cycle of the almond. It is the first tree to blossom, heralding spring. Its nut grows within a green fur casing, which splits open automatically. Hajo, Michel's nephew, collecting the nuts.*

Trees and Flowers on the Estate

The Mediterranean harbours a rich and diverse variety of plant life. I came here knowing precious little about any of it. A tree was simply a tree, aside from obvious exceptions such as the great British oak. I had never stopped to reflect upon the question of endemic plants, or otherwise. Plants grew. I liked them or I did not, and that was the sum total of it. Whether they originated from the region or elsewhere was not a question I thought to pose. But as I begin to learn a little about the complex and fascinating interlacement of Mediterranean cultures and history, and as I climb from bed each morning and look out of the French doors at the sun throwing shafts of burnished light across the top of the pine trees, listening to the

This fruiting cherry tree is one of two that came with the property. Opposite *The view from one of the higher terraces over the treetops to inland hills.* Previous pages *A magisterial old tree in our maritime pine forest.*

early morning birds in hearty voice, and as we ourselves begin to modify or change this patch of landscape by the choices we make with our planting, digging or extracting, I cannot avoid being drawn into the world of what subsists and grows all around me. And why.

The Mediterranean is small as seas go. It came about in millennia so far back that it does not bear imagining. Originally, there was a far greater sea called the Tethys, which ran from the Pacific to the Atlantic Oceans. Over the course of history this mass of water was expanding and contracting. The spreading and

shrinkage came about because thick heavy plates beneath the earth's crust were derailing, dislodging, drifting about in many directions. So violent were these seismic shifts that they caused the seabed to rise up and close in the land around them and create a smaller sea, the Mediterranean. Not only did this change forever the topography of the region, the build-up of lifting land mass, as one subterranean plate crashed and slid into and under another, created the fabulous mountain ranges that, today, encircle the Mediterranean. The region remains volatile geologically as the occasional eruptions of volcanoes such as Vesuvius, Etna, Santorini and others testify. Little more than a slender rim of arable land exists around much of the Mediterranean basin, where mountain ranges fall directly to the water's edge, which explains a great deal about the flora and fauna that survive here. Our little olive farm, approximately 100 metres above sea level, sits on limestone, once the seabed.

Opposite *The lane at the foot of our drive.* Left *A pear beneath the pool in blossom.* Above *A self-seeded Judas tree in full blossom.* Previous pages *One of our eucalyptus trees, flanked by oleander and yucca.*

Left *A lavender bank which we planted in the lower olive groves.* Opposite *Lavender in flower.* Previous pages *View of old Cannes, screened by a eucalyptus tree.*

The arrival of ice ages, wet spells and long dry periods, the migratory patterns of creatures whose food supplies were altered or cut off by climatic changes, all had a dramatic impact on the vegetation that began to spring up. Forests dominated these prehistoric wildernesses until man came along and began hacking them down for firewood, hut building, access. The oak, holm and cork (which needs more rainfall so is usually to be found a bit further inland) are believed to be two of the oldest surviving tree species along with, a little later perhaps, the earliest varieties of inedible wild olive. All three are widespread in these terrains. All are evergreens. Evergreens thrive here because of the hot dry climate, the extremes of weather. Loosely speaking, this is one of the reasons why it is said that the limit of the olive tree is the demarcation of the Mediterranean reach. It applies north into colder climates, and south into African deserts.

The olive tree is perfectly at one with the Mediterranean climate and soils – a symbiosis made in heaven (or from that prehistoric seabed) – and, in springtime, it sits in fields ablaze with colour from the wild flowers that shoot up around its feet, unless man intervenes, felling and spraying, disrupting the natural dynamics of the soil with fertilizers, disturbing the equilibrium, killing off plant life. Only the minimum of spraying takes place on our farm – none if I can help it – and we use no fertilizers whatsoever. So, in springtime, our terraces are a profusion of lipstick-red poppies, daisies, marigolds, blue starry borage, rosy bell-like garlic and tassel hyacinths, along with many others, most of which I cannot yet identify.

During those early years of extensive land clearance, we chopped down the holm oaks that were here when we purchased the property. I regret it now. One or two remain up in the pine forest, but it saddens me to think that we cleared away a variety of tree that has survived in this area longer than man. More, its acorns were one of primitive man's original foods.

Aside from the olive groves, our land is dominated by conifer stands that climb to the pinnacle of the hill. Cleanly scented as they are, and in spite of the cooling shade these towering softwood evergreens offer in the burning

Left *The bougainvillea, vibrant all summer long, climbs the villa's creamy façade.* Opposite *I planted the wistaria alongside the house about four years after we arrived. It has begun twining itself around the pillars along the walkway to the pool. In spring, its blossoming mauve racemes are a breathtaking sight.* Previous pages *Close up of the bougainvillea with a bumblebee at work.*

heat of summer, I had suggested that we chop them, replacing them with more olives, and then I began to pay attention to this maritime pine forest and to those whose habitat it is. There is history here. The trees when tapped bleed a deliciously scented resin. The Romans traded it. In the Middle Ages it was used for caulking wooden ships. The trees' bark extract is sold as a super health drug. These pines grow in Spain, France, Corsica and Morocco and support a wide diversity of wildlife, including eagles and owls. If we take them away, even to replace them with other trees, we will deprive many creatures of their nesting grounds, their homes. Others will come, of course, but even so…

Frequently planted in this neck of the woods is the Italian cypress, also known as Mediterranean cypress or Big Tree. We inherited a dozen or so, already mature. They are statuesque, sculpturesque, and a powerful green, which is all the more dramatic as they soar upwards in sharp contrast to the

cobalt sky. The Italian cypress is believed to be an authentically Mediterranean tree, probably a native of Greece and Turkey, possibly Syria and Libya, but curiously not of Italy. Astoundingly, it can withstand temperatures as low as –20°C.

One of my greatest joys when I step outside Nice airport after a trip away is to be greeted by the overwhelming scent of the peeling, thick-trunked eucalyptuses that adorn the alleyways alongside the car parks. When I breathe in that heady perfume I know that I am home. There exist over 700

Opposite *Wild growing white narcissi*. This page *Variegated tulips, camellia in a pot and (lower) passion-flower.* Previous pages *Plumbago, a fast spreading shrub, which can also be used as a climber. We have it trailing up through cypress trees. Blossoms in summer.*

species of gum tree as they are more informally called in mainland Australia and Tasmania, where they originate. Varieties of eucalypt were shipped back by the British at the beginning of the nineteenth century to adorn botanical gardens. Though they are not endemic, I am very fond of their subtle-toned leaves, as pale and delicate as *papier poudre*. Eucalyptus oil, extracted from the leaves, was held to be an efficient mosquito repellent, which was why they were planted in such profusion in wealthy Riviera gardens. An erroneous belief, although the oil is very effective in combating bronchial disorders. We have two eucalypts on the land. I cut swags from them and put them in the living room for their scent to pervade the open-plan space. However, it is a fact that their root systems can be invasive, lowering the water table and thereby damaging neighbouring vegetation.

We have planted bougainvilleas, mimosas, plumbagos, palms, bananas, mandarins, magnolias – and so the list goes on… none were originally Mediterranean plants. All have been brought from elsewhere to enhance this region's natural but more austere beauty, which they certainly do with their striking palette of colours and their exotic forms. I am exceptionally fortunate to be able to appreciate them on a daily basis, but I do sometimes wonder what effect over millions of years might these plant migrations have on our planet? Bees, for example, feeding off different pollens – are they evolving in some way that cannot yet be detected? Certainly their foraging habits are altering. These days, when planning new sections of the garden, our choices are more considered now that we have learned a little about the region, its indigenous flora and fauna and our earth's requirements.

Above *Dogs cooling in the pond. They ate all the waterlilies Michel bought us.* Opposite *The irises were growing wild everywhere on the land. We dug up a few and planted them in circles around the feet of the orange trees.*

Top *The cone-like fruits burst open in autumn, producing brilliant red waxy seeds.* Centre *The stunning white waxy flowers resemble teacups.* Bottom *Dried cones for the barbecue.*

Magnolia grandiflora

This tree is the belle of the ball. I noticed it when we first came to the property. I judged it magnificent then, but I had no idea what treasures lay in store. The Chinese have cultivated magnolias for 1,400 years. They are one of the oldest plant families in existence and fossils dating back 100 million years have been found. This species hails from the southern states of North America. It was first brought to Europe by the French botanist Charles Plumier. He shipped examples to France at the request of King Louis XIV who desired exotics for his gardens.

On Bastille Day of our first year, we drove overnight to revisit the farm. Arriving in a pre-dawn light, shattered from the road, we fell asleep in one another's arms on the concrete upper terrace. We awoke, stiff and hungry, soon after dawn to a fragrance that will forever remind me of love. The tree was in full waxy blossom. A spectacle that I will never forget.

An evergreen, it can grow to 27 metres tall, so ours is a third of the way there. Optimum seed production does not occur until the tree is well over twenty-five years old and because ours is a prolific seeder, and has been since we arrived, I calculate it is close to fifty.

The Ruin and Lost Vineyard

We did not find the ruin, which sits at the centre of the terraces that were once the vineyard, for quite some time. In earlier days it would have been a bothy, a shelter, for the vinekeeper. It would also have stabled animals, possibly donkeys, working as beasts of burden up and down the hillside.

Wild vines still shoot up on the surrounding land and we have allowed one or two to grow, to test the quality. They have fruited, but unlike the olive trees, the stock is poor. We intend to replant the vineyard at some point and will have to find a vine that thrives in this climate and limestone soil. Interestingly, I learnt from René that in France it is illegal to irrigate vineyards if the produce is to be sold commercially. Higher up the hillside on this section of the farm we uncovered another large water basin, so irrigation must have been possible. A wine variety expert came to inspect the grounds. He told us that the wine originally produced here would have been given to the land labourers instead of water. It was cheaper to produce!

The ruin had been buried behind herbage. Although walls have crumbled and we must rebuild it from scratch, parts of it have not been destroyed. The tiled floor, though filthy, remains intact and traces of the chimney are visible. Previous pages Spring field of wild flowers.

The Italian Stairway

Why did we christen it the Italin Stairway? I no longer remember. There is nothing particularly Italian about it. It was another joyous discovery when we cut back the land. We had been told that, somewhere, there was a ruin, but we knew nothing about this stairway. It sweeps from the base of the land to what must have been the original entrance to the house. Still, we felt it lacked structure. I suggested we pave it and found these lovely Bavarian white sandstone slabs, which Michel and Quashia laid. Running the length of it on either side Michel found rectangular hollows. 'There must have been a pergola here once upon a time.' He asked Jacques, our swimming pool expert, to design a series of arches, which Jacques did, and then we called in a blacksmith, Mr Poire, who built them in his atelier, delivered them and fitted them in a weekend. Michel has painted them this lovely soft green. The original plan was to plant up the arches with vines, but I think sweetly perfumed flowers will be more enticing.

Left *Three stages of the stairway.* Above *Aside from the planting, the stairway has been completed. Olive trees flank it at various levels. In autumn, when the olives are gathered, it is covered in nets.*
Below *A rare sight: the stairway brushed with snow.*

The Woodshed

Aside from the wood and glass cabin up behind the woodshed, all this construction work is Quashia's and he is exceedingly proud of it, as well he should be. In the early days, after land clearance, we had steres of cut wood. Some of it we sold to René but, aside from what we used for the barbecue and the fireplace, the rest lay for years, stacked beneath a holm oak, until it began to rot. A woodshed was required. Quashia built as far as the first three pillars, which

Left *The woodshed and walls as seen from the kitchen*. This page *Quashia at work. Rabbits breed in the log piles*. Following pages *Our woodstock shot through with evening sunlight*.

was more than sufficient for our needs. I had been moaning that the garage was crammed with rubbish and needed to be emptied in preparation for building works. During an extended absence of ours, Quashia took it upon himself to extend the woodshed and create what is now known as 'le hangar' as a storage space for all our gardening equipment. It took him an entire summer and broke our budget, but we are extremely glad to have it. I have planted fruit trees in front of it and jasmine to climb the wooden columns. In the evening when the sun's rays hit the honey-toned stones it is a remarkably beautiful sight.

Creating a Greenhouse

In the fourth century B.C., Plato observed that a seed could mature into a tree within a matter of days if kept in a 'garden of development'. However, there is little evidence to suggest that the Greeks, seafarers above farmers, experimented with plant propagation in elementary hothouses. The Romans, who dug pits and covered them with delicate crystal plates extracted from mica and talc, were probably the pioneers of this art. When the emperor Tiberius fell ill and his doctors prescribed a diet that included the daily consumption of cucumbers, his gardeners, aided by their rudimentary glasshouses, were able to provide him with his medicine on a year-round basis. For centuries after the Romans, the use of glass as an intensifier of heat and light was lost. It was not until the sixteenth century that the craft of glass-making really made headway.

*Irrigating and electrifying
the space proved remarkably
straightforward and
inexpensive.*

For a while, when I was a child, my parents owned a rambling Edwardian house
which boasted a delapidated greenhouse in the rear garden. Here my father stored
trunks of theatrical costumes, acquired from a bankrupted touring company, because
my mother refused to allow the 'moth-eaten finery' indoors. That conservatory
became my haven. I whiled away hours within it, with its broken windows and
warped door jammed ajar, dressing up, playing out my imagined scenarios of life
in eighteenth- and nineteenth-century orangeries. Our *serre* came about by accident.
When Quashia had finally completed his woodshed extension, an elongated strip
of stony land, not particularly deep but backed by an excellent stone wall, remained
alongside it. I suggested it might be the spot for a greenhouse. Michel telephoned
Mr Poire, the blacksmith, and construction of its cast-iron frame began in early
summer. However, the installation of the glass panes and reinforced roof sheets has
proved prohibitively expensive. Never mind, I idle away contented hours up there,
potting, sowing seeds, confident that at some stage my dream will see fruition.

Irrigation

There is nothing complicated about our irrigation system, because we do not have one. Even at this stage we work with buckets, or rather, extremely well-scrubbed plastic containers used to store chlorine tablets for the swimming pool, and miles of hosepipes. Watering is the bane of our lives. Between June and October we rarely see rain. Occasionally, if we are very lucky, there will be a spectacular thunderstorm with crashing and lightning that terrifies the poor dogs and sends them scurrying for cover in the stables, but otherwise the land is desiccated by the relentless heat, and the plants cry out for water.

We work in a relay system. I tend to do the pots around the pool and terraces, Michel attacks the flowerbeds, while Quashia handles the heavier loads. The hosepipes which, when joined together, can be from seventy to a hundred metres in length, are extremely heavy when transporting water. I have damaged the ligaments in both lower arms heaving them about, so have been obliged to retire from this chore. Fortunately the young olive trees require watering only once every three weeks.

Quashia is using the hosepipe, which straddles the length of the crown of the land, to fill a large container with water. From this he replenishes the small buckets, which he then empties at the feet of the small trees. It's very basic!

The Water Diviner

How much less irksome our irrigation commitments would be if we had a well.
It would also be more cost effective – water is very expensive in our commune.
The Belgian vendor of our farm had mentioned to Michel during those long-ago,
waterless days that there was a well on our land, but she could not remember
where it was or whether it had dried up. It is not indicated on our cadastral map
and we have never located it.

In order to register for agricultural water rates, which are less expensive than
standard household levels, we were obliged to call in a water diviner to confirm
that we had no private water sources. After initial surprise, I was rather taken with
the idea, thinking it an excellent guise for the support of vanishing trades. René
suggested that he knew just the chap and promised to bring him along to do a
recce if I agreed not tell anybody. I was bemused. It is not illegal to search for
water on one's own grounds, surely? In fact, according to our olive guru, water is
the only commodity, if discovered on private property, that the state entitles you
to keep. This was not René's concern. 'Claude', the water diviner, is a well-known
and highly esteemed man in these parts. It would not be done for everyone to learn
that he goes about searching for water.

'Claude' is orchestrating repair works for his water basin. René and 'Claude' consider the progress. Below *The largest water basin in the Alpes-Maritmes, 'Claude's' pumphouse.*

I had been expecting a chap '*du terroir*', of the soil, but instead a very
commanding gentleman zoomed up in a state-of-the-art American four-wheel
drive. He introduced himself in meticulous English – I recognized the name
instantly – then unpacked his divining rod. Within moments he claimed that he
could feel water. I was rather sceptical; we were standing by the swimming pool.

'Claude' found water at several different points, mostly beneath the reclaimed
terrace tiles which I have adamantly refused to dig up. Other water sources
farther up the hill proved impractical because the drilling lorry cannot gain
access to the sites. So, we are back to square one: irrigation of the groves with
buckets and hosepipes.

René and 'Claude' were boyhood pals who lost touch. When 'Claude' needed

Opposite *One of*
'Claude's' monumental olive
trees. Above *René standing*
in his broccoli patch.
Claude's olive harvesting
machinery.

someone to husband his olive farm he chanced upon the olive guru. Their
friendship was renewed; now they are inseparable. They proudly walk Michel
and me around 'Claude's' magnificent estate. 'We're 160!' he boasts, 'and we
run this place between us.' He possesses over 600 olive trees, and the pair of
them care for everything; no mean feat for two octogenarians.

'Claude' discovered two exhaustless sources of water on his property. He has
the largest water basin in the Alpes-Maritimes and never pays a penny in water
bills. It is crystal clear, *eau potable*, from mountain streams direct from the Alps.
And then we all trek to the shady terrace for a cool glass of champagne.
'Claude' only drinks champagne.

Dogs

When I was a child there were always dogs at home, as well as an assortment of animals on our Irish family farm where we spent our holidays. The woman who rented this villa before it was abandoned was a dog breeder, we learnt. I have often wondered if that left some lasting scent or trace that cannot be detected by us but gives the canine hordes a signal, because it is a fact that they turn up here regularly and move in. Occasionally, I have to give them their marching orders but more often than not I dole out delicious sustenance, which they gobble down greedily and, before we know it, we have another furry mouth to feed. Over the years, there have been those who breezed through, left their paw print and then moved on, while others have stayed the duration. Ella, our beautiful golden retriever, is the girl who springs to mind. I bought her as tiny puppy and she was with us until she died recently at the ripe age of almost sixteen.

Opposite *The puppies in my arms are those of our Belgian Alsatian, No Name, rescued by René and me.* Left *Lucky and Basset.* Following pages *'Dogs No Longer With Us'. I created this collage to celebrate the dogs who have shared our farm and afforded us so much happiness.*

No Name, the Belgian Alsatian, left her indelible mark. René and I found her, badly injured, in a clearing behind our hill. We hauled her back here. The vet cleaned her up and when he asked me her name I shook my head. No Name, I said, and it stuck. She delivered us nine puppies. Then one day she got up and walked away and I never saw her again. Every one has a story and has afforded us happiness.

Lucky

Of the trio who house with us now, Lucky is the senior. How she landed up here is quite strange. I was grieving the loss of my father. No Name had disappeared and I had recently purchased Ella, still a small puppy and suffering from lack of canine company. One morning, my father's birthday, I went to collect the post and there was Lucky sitting outside the gate, in amongst the irises, curled up in a ball. At first I thought she was No Name and then I realised that she was a smaller, different Alsatian. She snapped, would not let me near, but she was butted right up against our gate as though waiting to enter. I took the mail. She followed nervously, at a distance, up the winding approach. I piled high No Name's unused dish. She fed ravenously though only when I was out of sight. She was bald along her left haunch. Eventually, I got her to the vet who said that, skeletal though she was, she was carrying puppies. These we had to abort because she had been violently mistreated, kicked repeatedly. The vet warned me that she would never settle, never accept sharing a mistress with others. She had been traumatized. Lucky was a struggle. She was frightened, demanding, but now she has settled and is at home here. Hence her name.

Bassett

Bassett is a hunting dog, a tracker. He frequently skids up to the breakfast table, full of glee, tail a-wagging, with a warm rabbit swinging from between his jaws. We never allow him to keep his ill-happed victims. He hands them over without protest but watches on balefully, when we down coffee cups to give the furry corpses a decent burial. Unfortunately for Bassett, his antics wind up with calamitous results when he finds himself locked overnight in the cage intended to trap the wild boars or tangled within olive nets, but he never seems perturbed by these minor setbacks. He is a sanguine little fellow and devoted to his female companions. It was Lucky who first brought him here. I have no idea where from. During his first summer, when still a pup, he would lie with her on the terrace out of the hot sun, their limbs wrapped around one another, like lovers.

When he is not off hunting he sleeps, which is usually all day.

Lola

Lola is the junior of the family. I aquired her a short while after we lost Ella.
She belonged to a family who did not want her. It was Alexandre, our hunting
friend, who told us of her predicament. 'They will put her down...' For a few
weeks, it was a terrible struggle for Lucky until eventually she softened, yielding
to the arrival of Lola, comprehending that the younger animal was not her
enemy nor about to usurp her primacy.

Why anyone would want to dispose of a creature as beautiful as Lola was
beyond me, until she had been here a few weeks. She destroys anything she can
chew. She has eaten the nozzles and taps for every watering device we own.
She gets into the dustbins, dragging every scrap of rubbish all over the garden.
I buy her bones in abundance, synthetic as well as animal, but she tosses them
aside with disgust. Later, I will find the remains of flowers in plastic pots, awaiting
transplanting, strewn in shreds across the lawn. The second I exit my den, she
bats up like a possessed being and glues herself to my calf, knocking me over,
walking on my feet. She is young, Michel assures me.

Estate Neighbours

Gardens, old houses, flowers, stands of trees, are alive with different creatures. Most of them are not our enemies – aside from the wild boars! – and I try to live in harmony with them and not destroy them inconsiderately. Many have a way of life which suits our needs too. We have lizards aplenty, which we have attempted unsuccessfully to photograph, but they zip too swiftly along the terraces. They have remarkable camouflage abilities and occasionally, I will spot one hovering above the water in the pool. They never drown and seem able to negotiate the water's surface.

The brown geckos, a species of lizard, are hunters of insects so they stalk the walls in search of the flying or crawling beasties that might otherwise discomfort our lives. We have families of them. They live in the laundry house and behind the large shutters that close against the French doors. If in danger, they squeak. There is an array of birds, migrators as well as residents. I enjoy observing them, particularly the rarer species which I occasionally glimpse. Owls are a joy to encounter because, although we hear them on a nightly basis, they are very discreet. Certain eagles are more regularly sighted, as well as the more common birds of prey. Frogs give chorus to the night, croaking down by the streams in the valley while Barnabus, the elegant copper-eyed toad who lives within the flowerbed along side the garage, is a docile, inscrutable neighbour.

Above Barnabus, the oversized toad, who lives in the flowerbed alongside the garage. Left A praying mantis on the rose bush by the pool. Opposite One of the numerous families of geckos which share this house with us.

The Hunter

There is one creature trespassing on our land which is no longer welcome: the wild boar. These pigs are a plague in this district and are multiplying at an alarming rate. They cross over on to our terrain from the crown of the hill chewing access right through the wire fencing. They come at night in troops, usually led by a large sow, foraging the earth for bulbs and rhizomes, burrowing into the drystone walls for snails. They snap boughs and send walls tumbling in their wake. After they have passed through, the ground looks as though it has been churned by a bulldozer.

Alexandre is a friend who is employed by a local farmers' cooperative. He is a qualified hunter and licensed to use firearms. He offered to lend a hand. I refused, resisting all attempts to rid ourselves of these troublesome swine by aggressive means. The situation became more alarming when a

Opposite page *Alexandre hunting in the Alps with two comrades.* This page *Pictured with one of his beloved dogs and with his youngest daughter, Delphine.*

Wild boar damge to walls
and earth on our property. Two
young boars found on our land.
Opposite A newly born boar.
It looks so vulnerable!

neighbour's dog was fatally gored by a sow, followed by Quashia, the
restorer of the walls, threatening to down tools and leave. Michel advised
me that it was time to face reality. I relented and a caged trap was installed
on our land. For a brief spell the boars kept their distance only to return in
even greater numbers. The local council employ professional hunters to
send to distressed sites. I prefer to call on Alexandre who traps the boars
and then sets them free in the mountains where he hunts them legally.
He fosters the juniors – they cause the worst damage because they have
not learnt economy of effort – until they are sufficiently mature to fend for
themselves, then he releases them. A few he keeps for his family's kitchen.
Of those that are slaughtered, we are entitled to a share of the meat. It is
tradition and part of nature's cycle, but I cannot bring myself to participate.
Still, Michel and our guests enjoy these charcoal roasts.

Introduction to Honey Bees

Bee fossils discovered in amber have been dated back 45 million years. Bees were around long before man. During those gaping millennia the dominant species progressed from being a solitary insect to a participant within a tightly structured society. The operating system within beehives is, even today, cited as an ideal example of social harmony. When *Homo sapiens* eventually came on the scene they began to take interest in what bees had to offer. Aside from acorns and hunted game, honey was an early source of food for Mediterranean man. It came before olive oil. There are some splendid Mesolithic cave drawings in eastern Spain, and one in Valencia depicts two men collecting honey from an agitated nest of bees. Quashia has told me when, as a boy on the prowl for food for his family, he encountered a swarm of wild bees he would reach inside their nest and pilfer the honeycomb. Quashia and prehistoric Iberians may have been obliged to plunder from wild swarms, but the art of apiculture was practised in Egypt and Greece long before the written word. The earliest record of beekeeping in hives dates

Above *A visit to the beekeepers' chalet home.* Left *Hives in an alpine location and our beekeeper, François.* Opposite *Industrious workers on a frame. The hive is an arrangement of wax combs divided into cells. Here the bees store honey and pollen and rear young.*

back to approximately 2500 B.C. in Egpyt. The Greeks and Egyptians used bees' confections as both food and medicine. The ancient Greeks believed that Zeus was fed honey as a child, hence 'ambrosia', food of the gods, thought to bestow immortality. They were almost certainly the first to make the honey-based alcoholic drink known as mead, which they called 'nectar', the drink of the gods. Hippocrates, born 460 B.C., the 'father of medicine', praised honey's health-giving properties. Several centuries later, the Romans adopted the art of apiculture with such tenacity that it soon developed into a significant rural industry throughout their far-reaching Empire.

Michel and I are kitted up in protection suits. If the swarms are agitated when the hives are open, they sting. Below Michel has the wrong shoes! François lends him socks to protect his feet against stings.

We were keen to have hives, though we knew nothing about the art of apiculture. Michel suggested we find a professional interested in placing colonies with us in return for beekeeping lessons. The difficulty was that no apiarist accepted. Eventually, I received a call from Mr Huilier who had heard of our proposition through an apiarists' network. A fleeting introduction to him – his name translates as 'Oilcan' – led me to judge him a finicky fellow. Nothing could be further from the truth. He is passionate about his art and extremely knowledgeable. Until retirement he was a professional gardener, so his vast learning extends beyond his eusocial arthropods to their sources of food. He and his wife – they met later in life – built a chalet high in the Alps so they might indulge their two passions: mountain excursions and beekeeping.

Once the smoking apparatus, an enfumoir, *has calmed the bees, François pulls out frames. He confirms that the bees are healthy and collecting well. He points out the queen. Her silhouette is more elongated than that of her workers. She has been daubed with a coloured dot for instant recognition.*

Their house completed, they invited us to lunch and afterwards François drove us to an alpine clearing where dozens of hives were gathering from wild rhododendrons. Observing the hives in operation required opening them. For this, we donned protective suits – less easy than you might imagine! François prepared an *enfumoir*, an apparatus that creates smoke – he burns olive or pine kindling. Should the bees grow agitated when the hive is disturbed, they panic and sting. The scented fumes calm them. During these operations, François explained the rudiments of the honeymaking process.

Apis mellifera, 'honey-carrying bee' is the Latin name for the honey bee, but bees do not carry honey from blossoms to the hives. With their tongues they suck up flower nectar, which they transport back home. This sucrose-based

All these alpine plants can be found at up to 2,000 metres. The small orange flower is Lys Orangé or Lilium, a much rarer version of the common orange lily found in many gardens. The pink flower is Œillet dianthus. The yellow brush-like shrub growing amongst the stones is a member of the Hypericum family. Opposite The low red shrub is Rhododendron ferrugineum. It thrives at heights of up to 2,500 metres.

liquid is then passed from the collecting bees to hive-bound colleagues who regurgitate it and empty it into wax cells. Fellow workers flap their wings at an astounding rate to transform the consistency of the liquid into a thicker, stickier produce – honey. The cells when full are sealed with wax and the honey stored until winter. When the flowering season is over, nectar becomes scarce and the honey in the cells provides for the colony during the lean months.

Wild rhododendron honey, which is what these colonies were producing, is relatively hard to come by, but it is one of the specialities of our beekeepers. Fortunately, these shrubs grow in profusion close to their chalet.

Arrival of Bees at Home

It was an auspicious moment. We had been promised 600,000 bees in thirty hives – each containing 20,000 bees – but due to the serendipitous discovery of a wintering wild rose site, our beekeepers parked at the farm a mere 280,000 bees in fourteen hives. We gladly accepted those entrusted to us. Wooden pallets were laid on the ground to stabilize the hives. Each hive was marked with a coloured dot. This designates the age of the resident queen; she bears the same coding. The bees were scheduled to stay until spring, when they would be relocated to nectar-rich sites elsewhere. During the winter months, our apiarists visited regulary, confirming the well-being of the stock.

I lend a hand transporting hives. They were light, but in spring when chock-a-block with honey they can weigh up to eighty kilos apiece. Following pages *The hives at our olive farm during the dandelion season.*

All progressed smoothly until their penultimate visit when they discovered several dead colonies. I was devastated, assuming that, in some way, our terrain or we ourselves were culpable. I learnt then that European hives are dying off at an alarming rate. Two highly toxic insecticides used by farmers on sunflowers are believed by apiarists to be damaging the nervous systems of bees, thus destroying their innate ability to locate their hives.

Honey bees remain the dominant pollinators of flowering plants. In fact, in the long journey of evolution the role that these bees have played in pollination has changed the structure of plant life. We cannot underestimate their contribution in sustaining major ecological systems.

At Home

These are the precious moments: the days and evenings when we are alone, at home, working or enjoying time stolen from our demanding schedules. The interior of the house is used only occasionally during the long hot months when life is lived out of doors. The phone starts ringing. Friends, family would like to visit, and there is always a welcome. Michel and I are equally gregarious but perhaps in the long run I am the more solitary and, when I am at work on a project, quietude is essential to me. Whatever the weather, I work inside. I cannot concentrate in the heat and I need the library of books that surrounds me in my den. Michel, on the other hand, can happily type away in the dining room or beneath a parasol in the garden.

*Aspects of the upper level
of the villa. Michel
designed the open-plan
space. On this level there is
now only one bedroom, ours,
and there is no interior
staircase, so no matter how
numerous are the friends
staying we have our private
space. Following pages
Guest bedroom shutters
opening on to the pool.*

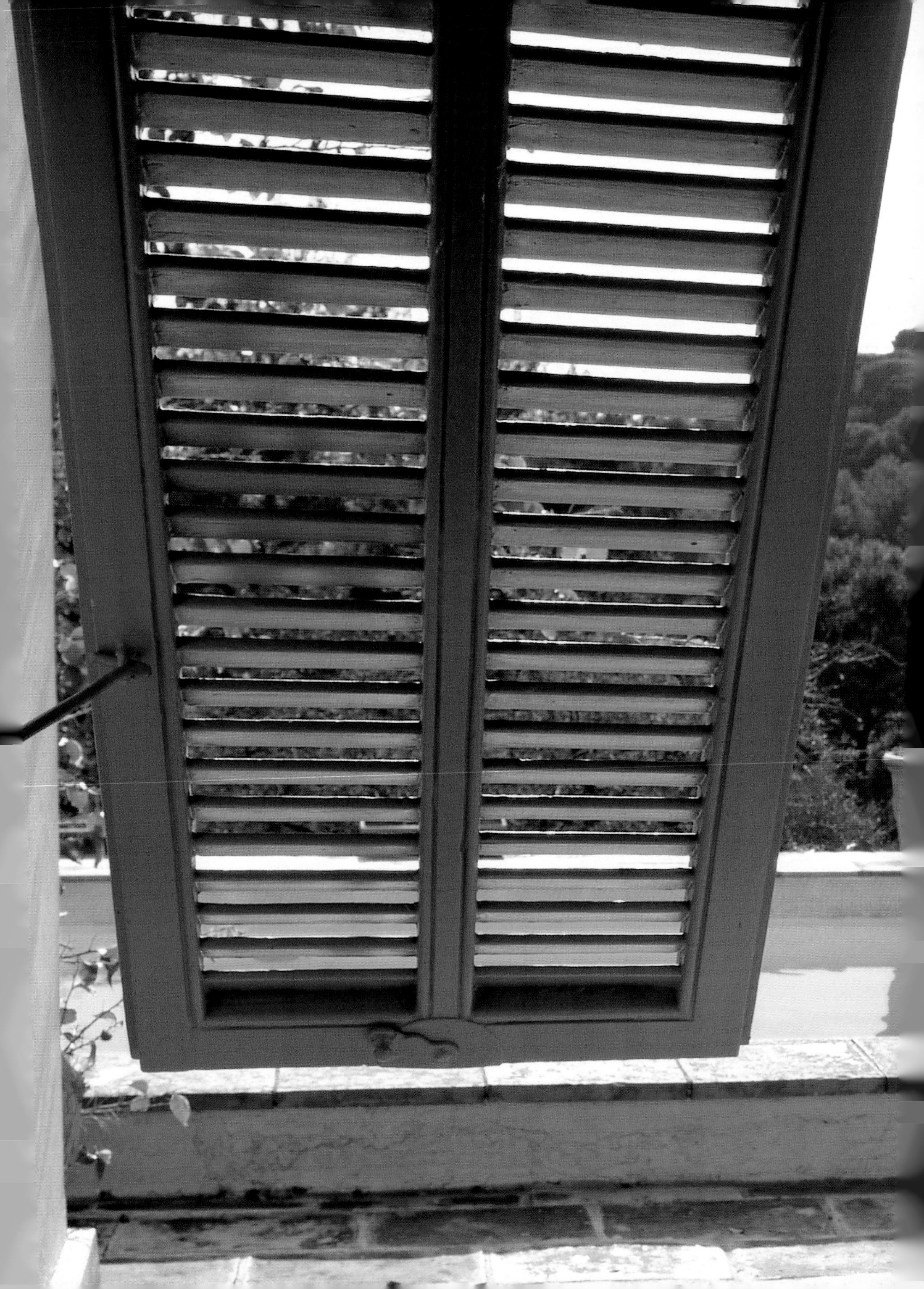

Outdoor Living

Here lies the hub of the house. On the terraces above and around the swimming
pool are tables, chairs, sunbeds, parasols aplenty. Simple furniture but chosen for
comfort and ease. Here is where the world congregates. Our good fortune is that
the grounds are extensive enough for everyone to be at peace, to be able to escape
or be engaged if that is their preference. While I am buried in my den, scribbling
away, I can hear the screams and splashes of children bombing in and out of the
pool. I can press my face against the glass and see others sleeping in the shade or
burning themselves silly in the sun. Because we are a multi-national family, with
several languages on the go at any given time, one of my secret pleasures is to
observe the cultural differences. Not always accurate, of course, but fun to note.

We have only one house rule at the farm and that is: make yourself at home.
We do not entertain in the conventional sense. Guests need to be able to look after

Life on the terraces. A kindly friend, Chris, deadheads the geraniums while a niece studies, feet in pool. Meals are shared. Life is celebrated. Following pages *A restful spot on the way to the upper house. The passion flower climbing the wall was the first plant I bought for the gardens.*

themselves because, although others might be on holiday, we are not. There are very few who do not find this arrangement easy to get along with. Downstairs, alongside the most spacious terrace where the long wooden table is situated, lies our summer kitchen. In winter, it is chock-a-block with oleiferous olives waiting to be pressed. In summer, the tall fridge is groaning with rosé and white wines, mineral water, goodies to nibble and meats to barbecue. Lunch is usually thrown together by whoever has the energy to deal with it. Not me, I am at work inside. Parties organize themselves to shop. Someone sets the necessaries in motion and by evening

when I am worn to a rag, some kindly soul has usually poured me a glass of wine. I breathe a deep, contented sigh and find myself a chair. The dogs saunter out from the shaded corners where they have slept the day away, while Michel is already up and at it, marshalling the barbecue team. After a sip, I will go and pick herbs for supper. We are preparing to share time with those we love. I don't have children – stepdaughters, yes – so those who surround me are my family. By evening, I am ready to unwind to the song of cicadas and crickets, the mellifluous jazz emanating from wherever and, together, we raise glasses and linger in one another's company.

The Pool

A secret: as a child my most precious dream was to go to Hollywood, to be a movie star and live in a house with a swimming pool. During the years I was traipsing the globe searching for 'My House by the Sea' I never envisaged it incorporating a pool. When we first set eyes on Appassionata, shabby and rundown as it was, the pool was a real added attraction. Living in this climate, the lack of one is disagreeable in the heat of the season. Still, we are enormously fortunate. It is an excellent form of relaxation during long and strenuous bouts of work. I also find tending the plants decorating its surround helps to clear my mind, but what gives me the greatest pleasure is the sharing of it. I love to see friends arrive after a long car journey and, almost before they have said hello, they hurl themselves into the water,

screaming like children. The real kiddies are endlessly happy splashing in and out of it. It is perhaps one of the few occasions when I allow myself the indulgence of regret. Regret that there is no child of mine to teach to swim, but that cloud passes almost as soon as it has been admitted and I laugh loudly watching others playing the fool. Clothes off, a pool is a great leveller.

Left and opposite *The pool shot from different angles in varying lights and seasons.* Following pages *A good time in the sunshine. A collage I made of friends and family on holiday.*

Moments of Tranquillity

It is the place itself, the environment, that sets the scene. Sea against sky:
turquoise against blue. Creeping changes in the light of day, the fall of
evening with its elongated shadows and burnt orange sunsets. Coppery
mornings. I close my eyes and listen to water tumbling into the pool; a tap
is turned on, plants are slaked; the dogs flat on their backs, legs in the air,
sighing in the heat; the birdsong; the distant Arabs calling the muezzin.
My breath, climbing the hill, heart beating, footfall against the spongy
pine-needled earth. Scent of resin. The crackle of olive wood in the
chimney. I have taught myself to preserve these moments. Freeze-dry
them. Stand still. For a time, for a while, back then, Michel and I went
our separate ways. I stayed on. Not easy. A heartbeat went missing.
Learning to walk the path of tranquillity, not loneliness. To find wealth
in the precious gifts and not to rage against the dying of…

This page *Michel dozing in
the hammock I brought back for
him from Brazil. Its colours are
identical to our shutters.*
Opposite *While the rest of us
swim and prepare lunch, Michel
walks an Australian friend
around the grounds.*

And then... Life went on. Returned. Changed. Returned. Wax candles
drip on to wood, guttering in the breeze. Rings of golden light encircle faces
across the plates. A barn owl hoots. Voices pause, fall into whispers, awed
by the darkness and nocturnal industry. Pablo Casals sawing strings, like
a black troubled bird. Someone uncorks a bottle. Have you seen the stars?
Heads are lifted. I glance across the table and lock the blue eyes of a man
who invited me into his life. He smiles, winks and turns his attention back
to the talking. Life is a series of these moments. Questioned. Stored. Like
squirrels in the almond trees. I close my eyes. Tomorrow, when he is snoring
in the hammock, I will climb aboard and sway gently at his side.

Snow at the Farm

Some years ago, it snowed here. It was St Valentine's Day. We were dining close
to the border of Italy. People rushed in off the street. '*Il neige, il neige,*' they were
exclaiming. The proprietess, a bottle-blonde Mama, scurried to an imposing dresser,
grabbed a fistful of photographs in an elastic band, sepiad with age, like fading
postcards and ran from table to table, waving them. 'My restaurant in snow!'
That night, the journey home was treacherous. Skidding and sliding, the car perched
terrifyingly at the cliffside. My mother was with us. I could hear her whimpers.
We arrived at dawn, safe but shaken.

Snow is such a rare occurrence here. This year it came during harvest. We were
working in the sunshine, warm from exertion and the benign temperatures. The next
afternoon, Sunday, it was snowing. 'It's snowing,' I cried. Michel laughed. 'It won't
settle.' 'We'll have to stop the harvest if it does.' 'It won't settle.' But it did.

Left *The top of the
Italian staircase, looking
down to the ancient olive
groves.* Opposite *The
young apple trees I planted
in memory of my father
and, beyond, the Italian
cypresses. Snow, this close
to the coast, is exceptional.*

The snow has settled and, in spite of the warm sunny temperatures, it has begun to turn icy. I love this image of the sun loungers covered in crystallizing snow.

3 *Beyond the Farm*

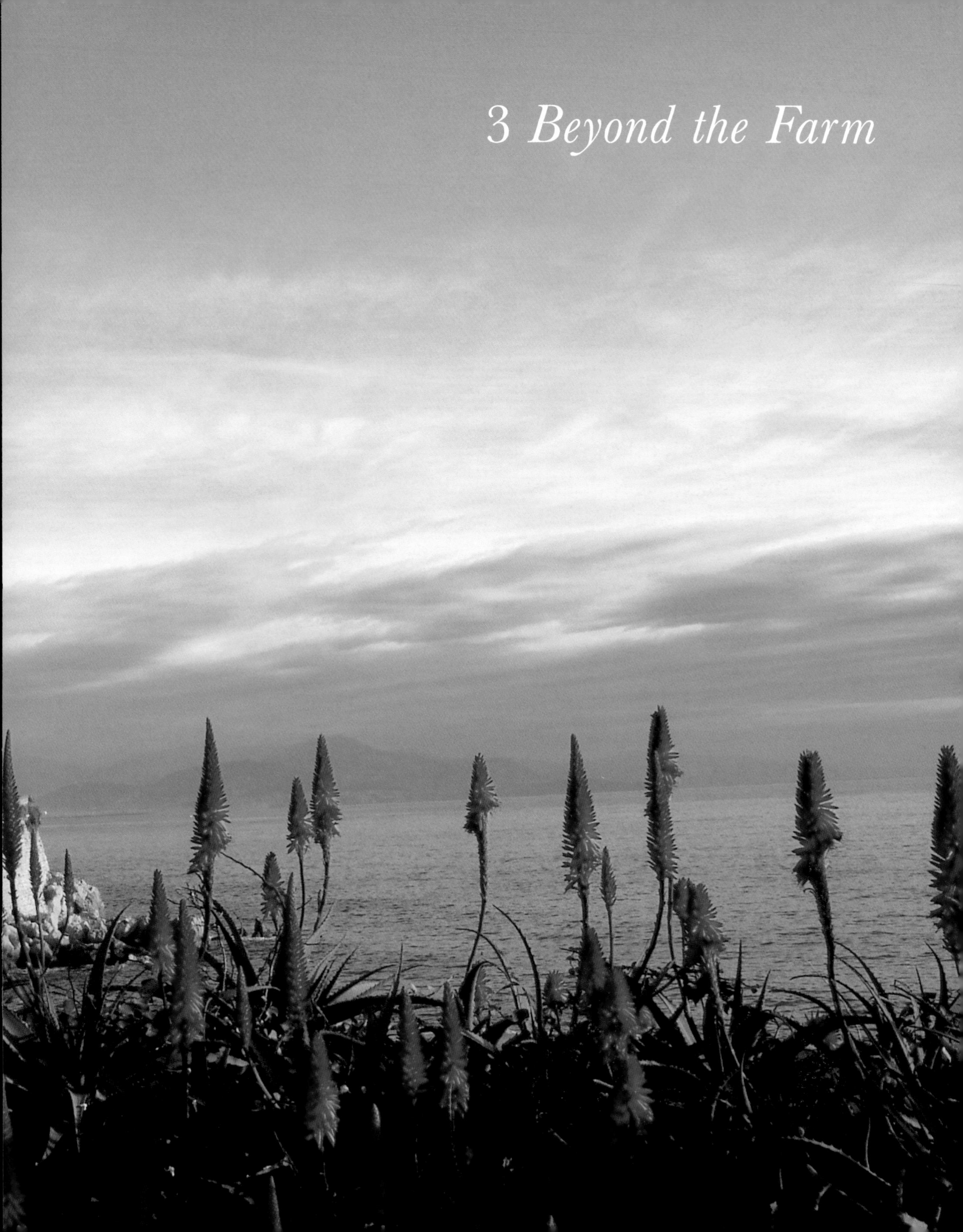

The Matisse Chapel at Vence

In 1941, the French painter Henri Matisse fell seriously ill. His night nurse at his home in Cimiez above Nice was unavailable. In her absence, a twenty-one-year old, Monique Bourgeois, was despatched. She had just lost her father in the war and had never heard of Matisse. He was estranged from his wife of many years and Monique became his model, his friend. Their story over the ensuing years is a remarkable one, which finds its culmination in his last great masterpiece, the Chapel at Vence. Monique took vows as a Dominican nun, assuming the name Sister Jacques-Marie. It was almost by accident they conceived the chapel – a drawing of hers that inspired him, and they set to work.

The first time I saw the Chapel of the Rosary, the day after Michel and I had first visited Appassionata, it was closed. We stood in the road, jumping high, eager to see, to catch glimpses of the garden with its sweeping views to the sea. Michel drew my attention to the spire with its iron cross standing almost thirteen metres high. And to the roof itself, tiled in azure against an azure sky. It was so unlikely, yet immaculate symmetry.

'We'll paint the shutters the blue of Matisse's roof,' Michel said. I closed my eyes and pictured it. Against vanilla walls. Yes, it would be perfect.

Above *The chapel with its view to the Mediterranean with the spire and iron cross on the roof. Even without the bell, its weight was such that there were difficulties in securing it.* Below *Stained glass window in the chapel.* Opposite *The iron cross standing thirteen metres high. Matisse envisaged it as a beacon to be seen from far and wide.* Opposite right *A tiled relief above the entrance door.*

Visit to the Island of Saint Honorat

I have two favourite spots along the Provençal littoral. To these
I disappear to blow away the cobwebs. The first is a hop across the
water, to the Îsles de Lérins (originally known as Lero and Lerina). In
particular, I prefer the more southerly isle of St Honorat. A forested
idyll, it is a world away from the commercialism of much of today's
Côte d'Azur. Once upon a time, in what was not yet unified France,
the island was a centre for retreat and teaching. Officially, it carries
the title St Honoratus after its religious founder, the Trier-born
playmate of the future Roman emperor, Flavius Gratian, who gave up
all political ambitions when he converted to Christianity, from whence
he became a significant figure in the early Western Christian Church.
It is claimed that St Patrick studied at St Honorat on his journey

Opposite *Cannes in the distance as we speed towards the islands. I am staring out towards the southern reaches of the Mediterranean from the fortified monastery.* Left *The* monastère fortifié, *fortified monastery. The original* donjon *was begun in 1073 to protect the monks against invasion. What is striking about the building is its elegant, simple form.*

The public entrance to the nineteenth-century church adjoining the cloister where the Cistercian monks reside. The island of St Honorat has been inhabited by monks almost without interruption since the fifth century A.D.

Above *Palm trees shadow
the entrance to the church within
the abbey grounds.* Below
*The abbey seen from an upper
level of the fortified monastery.
The views from here across the
Alps and along the coast are
breathtaking.* Opposite
*The sun setting across the
Mediterrean. Time to go home.*

north to Ireland. Today, it is home to a tiny community of industrious Cistercian monks. Alongside the rigours of their spiritual life, they husband olive groves and vineyards and sell honey from their hives. Lerina, their homemade liqueur, contains properties distilled fom forty-four different herbs. Theirs is a silent order and they request respect during visits to their monastery and nineteenth-century church.

We take the boat from the old port in Cannes, an invigorating twenty-minute excursion, which lands us in the island's pine-scented quietude. A hike round the water-lapped acres takes about an hour. We linger. There are seven chapels to vist, shaded alleys flanked by Aleppo pines to stroll along, stone benches for rest and meditative reflection and bays from which to eulogize the view and swim.

The Camargue

The Camargue is a delta, a sprawling expanse of flat land, ringed in by two estuaries which flow south to the sea like the open arms of a yearning lover. These lesser waters, forking from their mother source, the Rhône, are known as the Grand Rhône and the Petit Rhône, and in between them lies this fabulous, mysterious, croissant-shaped delta where native white horses and solid black bulls roam as freely today as they have since prehistory. Nature here is windswept, reedy, caney. There are salt pans – this is France's largest salt-producing area – marshes carpeted in spongy samphire, grasslands, lakes and, at its coast, sandy dunes and beaches. It is a labyrinth of grassland and golden-hued swamps and, to me, it is one of the most uplifting places on earth.

Less than two hours drive from our stone-terraced olive groves, it is a world away from any other *département* of Provence. Gone are the fertile hills, the valleys, vineyards and olive groves, gone are the mountains that plunge to the sea. Here is wild nature where little besides rice and a vine first planted by the Romans and cultivated in

This page and opposite *The pink flamingos are everywhere in the Camargue. The chicks' down is grey. It is in adulthood that they take on this magnificent colour.* Previous pages *There are few stands of trees in the Camargue. Those available are used as nesting grounds for the herons. It is a magnificent sight. Colonies of these birds, flapping great wings, wheeling in the wintery sunlight. Eight species of heron frequent this delta.* Following pages *Marshy waters in the bird sanctuary.*

sand thrives. Owing to the area's excessively saline atmosphere, there are precious few trees, just a few random figs; lonely, desolate silhouettes gnarled by weather.

A trip to this region is one I usually make alone, a pilgrimage to the birds, to the ornithological park on the outskirts of the coastal town of Saintes-Maries-de-la-Mer. Birds are wheeling and whistling everywhere. Harriers and songbirds overhead and lanky waders strutting and plodding in the silty waters. The most famous, of course, are the huge flocks of pink flamingos (*Phoenicopterus ruber*). I never tire of watching them, but when they take flight

they leave me breathless. Their lipstick-pink wings, rimmed with black, beating silently across the blue heavens. Many flocks winter in the Camargue but in late September thousands take to the air, commencing their migration south to Africa, some as far as Senegal. It is worth the journey to the Camargue to sit cross-legged on the ground and watch them cross the firmament.

The famous white horses of the Camargue are actually born brown and gradually turn white after five to seven years. Today, they are almost all privately owned and branded but, apart from the few used for tourist rides, are left to roam wild. The local black bulls, or *bouvines*, are smaller than their Spanish counterparts and many are rounded up to take part in the local bullfights, *courses Camarguais*, which involve trying to pluck coloured ribbons from their horns.

White horses and back bulls have lived in this region since time immemorial. The Camarguais tame them and use them for their farming and bullfighting but, unlike the Spanish corrida, *no blood is shed in the Camargue bullrings. Man and nature are in harmony here.*

Above *The old town of Antibes. The port of Antipolis was probably founded around the same time as Marseille, Massalia, six hundred B.C.*
Left *Aloes in flower.*
Opposite *From the ramparts of the old town, looking west.*
Previous pages *View from the west across the Mediterranean to the old town of Antibes. In the distance are the Alps.*

Antibes

Antipolis, the original name for Antibes, means 'city opposite' in Greek. Both Marseille and Antibes would have been strategically important coastal settlements for the Greek and Roman fleets. It is unclear whether the Greeks intended its appellation to mean opposite Nice, Nikaia, or the island of Corsica. Here we are in Picasso country – the town hall offered the artist a spacious atelier with magnificent views across the ramparts to the sea. Today, it is the Musée Picasso – and Graham Greene land. I used to see Mr Greene at regular intervals outside Chez Felix where he and I would be waiting for the arrival of the British newspapers. In fact, I would journey there in the hope of glimpsing him, hero that he was to me. After a glass or two of rosé, he became quite chatty with customers, leaning in with mischievous blue eyes, 'How's the fish, good?' It amused me that no one recognized him. Once, I saw him dancing with a fire hydrant down by the port.

Above and left *It is rare to meet young men still working with flocks. This fellow tells us that he shares the work with his cousin. Originally, it was his father's business.* Opposite *After the grape harvest, the plants are inspected and pruned.* Following pages *From the island of St Honorat, looking towards Cannes and the Alps.*

A Hazy Day in the Var

The Var is the neighbouring *département* to our Alpes-Maritimes. We drive to the vineyards, stopping at either a family-run domain or a local village cooperative to buy wines. Although this region is not as renowned as Bordeaux or Burgundy for its viticulture, it is fast building a reputation, particularly for its rosés. A visit in late autumn when the foliage is turning red and yellow is spectacular. During this season, the people of the *terroir*, of the soil, are hard at work. After the grape harvest, the stock is inspected. If the leaves turn too rapidly, it signals that the roots have been attacked by a fungus. These plants are swiftly removed before the mould spreads, burnt and replaced with young vines. It is labour intensive. An acre of land requires up to 2,000 plants.

The sheep pasture in the mountains during the summer and are driven down from the high plains in October; they stay in this more benign climate until May. During this period they are inspected, innoculated and sheared. Shepherds are a dying breed – the work is not financially rewarding. Although, traditionally, it remains a family affair, the young men go to the cities, to seek more lucrative employment.

Recipes

These are a few of the recipes I have learnt since moving to the land of the Mediterranean Diet. Olive oil is fundamental to all, except any sweet dishes, of course. Mealtimes are a celebration of what is in season.

Oil of Fennel

In restaurants all along our Mediterranean coast you will find on the menu variations on *loup*, sea bass, baked in a papillote of tinfoil. Usually, beneath the fish there are longish stalks of dried fennel. Fennel is an exceptionally easy herb to grow. Even without my attention it sprouted dramatically in the patch of land behind my London flat. Here, at the farm, we keep several plants in the vegetable garden. The traditional date for harvesting it is 29 September, the feast of St Michel. After a long dry summer the plants are tall and stringy, with plate-like heads of yellow flowers and seeds. Each year, around the feast of St Michel, we gather our fennel plants, cut them into small branches as though ready for a vase, slide them into elegant glass bottles and pour our olive oil in until the umbels are submerged. We set the sealed bottles aside in the cool shade of the summer kitchen until the end of November. This gives the fennel time to infuse the olive oil. After those few weeks, we leave the oil on the table to be used whenever fish dishes or certain vegetable crudités are served. It adds a subtle piquancy that is truly delicious.

Scrambled Eggs with Wild Asparagus

10 free range eggs
1 large bundle of asparagus
1/2 cup of extra-virgin olive oil
Sea salt, black pepper

At home and all around our area in southern France asparagus grows wild on the hills. (The wild asparagus shoots can just as easily be replaced with the regular varieties but choose the fine rather than thick varieties.)

Our Arab gardener pointed the delicate spears out to me and I picked and cooked some, but I found the taste far too bitter. Now that I have found this little recipe I do serve it occasionally, but I tend to opt for market-purchased asparagus produced by one of the many *maraîchers*, market gardeners, working in the hills all about here. Cut the asparagus into delicate chunks, throwing away the hard, last third of the vegetable. Place the rest in a pan of extra-virgin olive oil and heat, turning regularly. Break the eggs, mix with salt and pepper and pour the mixture in with the oil and asparagus and leave until it's cooked. However, be aware that this dish is at its best if it is served runny and not allowed to overcook or become a thick paste. Serve immediately.

Provençal Tomatoes

2 large tomatoes for each person
4 garlic cloves
lashings of olive oil
Sea salt, black pepper, fresh parsley and chives

Cut the tomatoes in two and spoon out the seeds. Pour olive oil into the pan and place the tomatoes, cut side down, in the oil. When the watery liquid has drained, turn them, salt them, pepper them, and leave them to cook on a very low heat for about three-quarters of an hour. If they begin to dry add a small amount of water and a spoonful of oil.

Ten minutes before they are done, add to each halved tomato a garlic clove, chopped parsley and chives.

We eat this very simple dish with wholegrain, wild rice from the Carmargue or as an accompaniment to grilled lamb chops. Serve in summer with a Bandol rosé or a chilled Côte de Rhone red. Any reader who adores rice and is travelling through southern France might be interested to know about the rice festival in September at Arles.

Tapénade

This is the famous spread made from olives. It is quintissentially Provençal. The name itself comes from a Provençal word, tapé, *which is the fruit of the caper.*

10 anchovy fillets
2 cups of pitted, French brine-cured
black olives.
1 tablespoon of drained capers
1 teaspoon of Dijon mustard
1 peeled garlic clove, finely pressed
$\frac{1}{2}$ teaspoon fresh thyme. Use only the leaves.
$\frac{1}{8}$ teaspoon mixed dried herbs of Provence
Freshly ground black pepper
$\frac{1}{2}$ cup of extra-virgin olive oil
Many true Provençals also like to add a shot
of Cognac

Desalt the anchovies by running them under the tap. Take out the small central bone and cut them into morsels. Dry the capers. Put the chopped capers, olives and anchovies together with the finely chopped garlic. Add the herbs and the teaspoon of mustard. If using Cognac, now is the moment to add it. Begin to press the ingredients into a paste. While mixing and thickening the paste, add the extra-virgin oil. (These days many cooks use a food processor.) Or it can be done, old-fashioned style, with a pestle and mortar. The main thing is that the paste is smooth. It is quite delicious served with grilled toasts or lightly salted biscuits, finely sliced cucumbers, tiny crottins of goat's cheese and a chilled apéritif on a warm summer's evening.

Tapénade can also be spooned in with fresh, warm pasta.

Figs stuffed with Tapénade

Make a slit in the side of each fig and spoon about half a teaspoon of tapénade into the fig. Pinch the opening closed. Attach a sprig of mint to each fig and serve. Delicious served with a small glass of chilled sweet white wine and a helping of fresh goat's cheese.

Casserole of Wild Boar

Dice the meat (choose rump meat, if possible) of the boar into cubes and place them into a generous-sized bowl. Slice 2 leeks, 2 carrots and 2 onions into the bowl. Add a palmful of dried herbs, chopped fresh chives, three-quarters of a bottle of reasonably full-bodied red wine (I use a Bandol) and three teaspoons of olive oil. Season with sea salt and black pepper. Loosely cover the dish with a clean tea-towel and place in a cool dark place to marinate for twelve hours.

Gently heat 2 sliced garlic cloves and a few herbs in olive oil and, just as the mixture is getting warm, add the marinated chunks of meat. Allow these to cook gently until the meat has browned. In a separate pan, also with olive oil and herbs, fry the marinated vegetables. Pour both meat and vegetables into a pre-heated terracotta oven dish, add the marinade, two teaspoonfuls of brandy, black pepper and sea salt and slide it into the oven to cook on a slow heat, 180°C/350°F/Gas Mark 4, for three hours. This recipe can also be adapted to venison or goat.

Wild Boar Spit-Roasted or Barbecued

A renowned authority on the science of human metabolism and nutritional aspects of diabetes was approached by the French national federation of hunters to study the nutrional values of six popular game meats: pheasant, partridge, hare, buck and doe venison and wild boar. Professor Ducluzeau declared that all these hunted game foods are organic meats. They are rich in potassium and phosphorous as well as iron and easily digested by humans. They are less fatty than the average yoghurt and the fact that these animals, unlike reared stock, are constantly on the move, frequently running and changing location regularly, well-exercised and feeding naturally, makes their meat the healthiest to consume.

Spit-roasting a whole beast is only worth embarking upon if you are intending to entertain a minimum of twenty guests, so this is a dish we save for parties. While the fire is being prepared, we stuff the pig with a dozen apples and a kilo of pork stuffing and sew him up again. Two important factors that affect the taste of the cooked beast: the first is the wood used for the fire – we tend to use pruned olive and green oak branches – and the second is to be sure to baste the animal regularly with an olive oil and herb dressing. As the beast turns on the spit, to keep its skin from drying and splitting, brush it regularly with the olive mix using as your brush twigs of freshly picked rosemary. The ideal length for the sprigs is about 25 centimetres.

Dandelion Leaves in Salad...

We regularly eat the leaves of young dandelions in our salads. They are famously rich in iron and very good for the circulation. The young *pousses* are found in the mixed salad known here as *mesclun*. *Mesclun* is a derivation of the Niçois word *mescla* which means mixing, blending. In earlier days the famous *mesclun* was made up purely of green leaves from a variety of local herbs (parsley, chervil, dill) and plants – rocket, purslane, watercress, endive or broad-leaved chicory, cos lettuce, lamb's lettuce – but, today, red salads are frequently added. We follow the French tradition and serve the salad after the main dish. It helps to cleanse the palate for the cheese and desserts still to come. This aromatic collection of leaves needs little dressing and is best served with a little olive oil, a squeeze or two of lemon and a couple of pinches of sea salt.

....and its Flowers as Jam

I came across this in a dog-eared book of traditional southern French recipes I picked up at a local brocante *(junk shop). When spring is in the air and the fields are filled with flowers, take a basket and go a-gathering. Choose a sunny day; you will need patience and several hours in the fields because this recipe requires the full-blossomed heads of three hundred and fifty dandelions!*

Back at the house wash them thoroughly, be careful not to damage them, and then drain them, spreading them out on a flat dry surface and leave them for twenty-four hours. When they are ready, prepare one and a half litres of water, flavoured with the juice of two lemons and two oranges (freshly picked, if possible). Add to this the dandelion heads and leave the mixture to boil in a saucepan. Once boiled, turn off the heat and leave it to cool. Then filter the juice, weigh it and add to it an equal weight of sugar. Cook the mixture in a thick-based pan for about forty-five minutes or until it has the consistency of a richly golden liquid honey. Pour it into jars and leave, sealed. Serve on toast or freshly baked bread with steaming coffee for breakfast. Or try our secret: pour a spoonful of it into natural yoghurt instead of honey. Delicious!

Oysters Recipe

I swallowed my first oyster in my early twenties in a rather smart brasserie in Knightbridge where I was dining with the late, great Hollywood movie mogul, Sam Spiegel. 'I love oysters,' I lied, grinning flirtatiously. Though I was behaving, I thought, in a frightfully grown-up, woman-of-the-world manner, I was secretly shocked at the price, which even then was about £15 a dozen! As with all unforgettable moments, such rites of passage leave indelible marks and, for me, oysters became the astronomically expensive or deliciously decadent fare of movie stars and moguls. Cocaine, Montrachet and oysters: a Hollywood–New York club of which I knew so little but to which I craved entry.

Oysters, *les huîtres*, flood the streets of France at Christmas and are an essential aperi-dish for both year's-end festivities. But here's the difference. In France, oysters are a food for the people, they are everywhere and oh, so cheap. Here along the coastal drags of the Côte d'Azur and in the cobbled perched villages, somewhere around mid-December fishmongers set up marquées on street corners and at these arrive, on a daily basis from *oestriculteurs* in Brittany and Normandy, dozens of freshly packed balsa-wood boxes of *huîtres* nestling in layers of spongy, sludge-brown seaweed. Whatever takes your fancy is on offer: *Fines de claires*, which is the staple of the French oyster market; *Speciales de Marennes*; *huîtres creuses* (rock oysters); *Speciales de claire* (*claire* translates as a clear pond or a fattening pond for oysters); juicy *belons* with their flatter, less corrugated

shells; *Speciales de Normandie…* the list is long, salty and delicious. Supermarkets sell oysters in boxes of three dozen and, depending on what you choose, you can expect to pay somewhere between 18 and 20 Euros for the lot. There is the famous old adage that one should only eat oysters in months with an 'r' in. In fact, this is not necessarily true. It has come about because in the summer months the oysters are *laiteuse*, milky, and of a thicker consistency. They contain eggs, which makes them fleshier. Some find this texture a little unpleasant but it is not uncommon for them to be eaten in France during these months. It is simply a question of taste, though they also need to be eaten very fresh to avoid them going off in the heat. They are often served with a shallot vinegar, but we eat ours, shucked at home, cooled on ice and sprinkled with fresh lemon juice from fruits from the garden.

Schile Agio e Ogio

This is a traditional Venetian dish, is extremely simple and enhances any summer lunch in the garden. Our version is loosely based upon the original.

Using 6 prawns per person, freshly peel them and submerge in a pot of sea-salted water. Heat until there is a good froth. Then remove the prawns, drain them and place them in a deep pan with 3 tbsp of extra-virgin olive oil, 3–5 freshly sliced garlic cloves, 2 finely chopped shallots, chopped parsley, chopped chives, black pepper. (We cheat and add fresh thyme and rosemary, which gives the dish a Provençal twist.) Cook over a fierce flame for a few moments – on special occasions, the Venetians add 2oz brandy: pour it over the shellfish, set light to it and cook for a minute until flames have burnt out.
Serve sizzling to the table, with half a lemon for each plate. Tear a chunk off a fresh baguette and dip it into the warm, herby oil. If you prefer, you can serve the prawns with rice. A well-chilled crisp white wine is its best accompaniment.

Vin d'Orange

This is Alexandre's recipe, not René's, who adamantly refuses to disclose his secrets. It will produce 10 litres of vin d'orange. This is a typically Provençal pre-dinner drink.

4 sweet oranges
4 bitter oranges
1 lemon
10 litres of white wine or rosé, whichever you prefer
2 litres of eau de vie
4 sticks of vanilla
4 sticks of liquorice
2 kilos of loose brown sugar

Steep the ingredients for forty days and then filter.
Serve as an apéritif direct from the fridge and without ice cubes.
Personally, I find the taste of vanilla a little dominating so we add only 2 sticks.
Another alteration of ours to Alexandre's recipe is to add a lime as well as a lemon. We serve our *vin d'orange* with champagne (or bubbly white wine), a mix of ¾ champagne and ¼ *vin d'orange* – it is delicious.

Acknowledgements

This book includes glimpses, fleeting and intimate, into the lives of many members of our families and our friends. I would like to thank each and every one for agreeing to share with me and my readers moments of their story. Also to those who have lent us snapshots from their personal albums, your generosity has enriched the pages. Michel's contribution has been inestimable. He has combed the land at all hours in search of the perfect light, the unexpected shadow. A rare and special partner, he is. To him I say, I love you. You make the difference.

This book would not have happened without Michael Dover of Weidenfeld & Nicolson Illustrated who read my Olive trilogy and felt sufficiently enthused to make an offer. Michael, as both publisher and editor, has been a fine eye and splendid support. The design team for this work are David Rowley and Clive Hayball. They have given so generously of their time and expertise and I am deeply grateful, to Robbie Polley for an enticing drawing of the layout of our little farm and to Jennie Condell for being a smiling link. Within the Orion Publishing group are a body of people who move like an industrious army to get the books publicized and into the shops. To you all, I am indebted. Susan Lamb and Alan Samson, you are pole stars. Lastly, to my splendid agent, Jonathan Lloyd at Curtis Brown and his girls, Camilla and Alice. *Merci beaucoup à tous.*

First published in Great Britain in 2005
by Weidenfeld & Nicolson
10 9 8 7 6 5 4 3 2 1

Text copyright © Carol Drinkwater 2005
Photographs copyright © Michel Noll & Carol Drinkwater
Design and layout © Weidenfeld & Nicolson 2005

A CIP catalogue record for this book is available from the British Library.

ISBN 0 297 84404 0

Design director: David Rowley
Designed by Clive Hayball
Illustration by Robbie Polley

Printed and bound in Italy

Weidenfeld & Nicolson
The Orion Publishing Group Ltd
Wellington House
125 Strand
London, WC2R 0BB

Page 1 *Blue-gated entrance to our olive farm.*
Pages 2–3 *From behind villa to the Mediterranean.*
Pages 4–5 *Looking towards villa from the ancient olive groves.*

Photographs on pages 15, 102, 197 (bottom right) by David Rowley